The Savior's Path

Tracking the Mysterious Footsteps of Jesus

(Signposts Provided)

by Lynnelle Pierce

Lynnelle Pierce
11541 N. Lake Drive
Holland, MI 49424
© 2012 Lynnelle Pierce

ABOUT THE AUTHOR

Lynnelle Pierce is a Bible teacher to hundreds of women in West Michigan. Her love for God's Word spills out of her soul and into her studying, writing, and teaching. She believes with all of her heart that the Bible is the ONLY Book that is relevant, alive, and communicates to anyone who has a desire to "hear" from the Lord, Himself.

Lynnelle simply cannot get enough of Jesus. As she studied the Gospels, she developed a curiosity and longing to know how Jesus "got here." That's what prompted her to dig into the Old Testament, and she discovered the mysterious steps of Jesus all through those 37 books. To her, it was an illumination of how the Old Testament became the New Testament. It was worth the study!

Lynnelle and her husband Tom live in Holland, Michigan. They have two married sons and five grandchildren.

Lynnelle has authored four other books:

Have You Heard About That Fruit?
God's Gals Haven't Changed a Bit
What God Says, He Does
Prayer, the Heart Changer and Mountain Mover

This book was written after much prayer and study.
During that long process, there were four precious spiritual sisters
who stood in the background.
They listened, encouraged, and loved me through it all.
So, with a grateful heart, I dedicate this book to:

Mary Breuker
Hilda Dixon
Ruby VanderPlow
Gerta Vink

James 1:17: *Every good and perfect gift is from above, coming down from the Father of the heavenly lights, who does not change like shifting shadows.*

THE SAVIOR'S PATH

Tracking the Mysterious Footsteps of Jesus

TABLE OF CONTENTS

INTRODUCTION

It all started as I watched our son and daughter-in-law cross the finish line of the Disney Marathon. I saw their facial expressions of such accomplishment, and I also saw the gold Mickey Mouse medals that were placed around their necks. I wanted one of those medals. There was no way that I could jump the fence and fake it, and I knew officials were not handing them out to just anyone. The only people who were privileged to get Mickey Mouse medals were those who ran the race—those who worked hard to prepare and got themselves ready for such a challenge.

The thoughts that went through my head were natural ones: don't even think about it; it's out of your realm of possibility. Our son, in the course of our week there at Disney World, heard me asking questions of various people I saw who had run the race. He asked me if I wanted to run in it the next year. I laughed and said there was no way I could ever run 26.2 miles at my age. My place was standing at the finish line with their three children cheering them on as they ran. He assured me that I could do it. For Mother's Day that year, he signed me up and paid the registration fee—nice kid, right? He told me that I just needed a nudge, and he was going to give me that nudge because he knew then I would pursue it and begin the long, grueling, step-by-step, day-after-day, week-after-week, month-after-month training.

Now, I could have done the half-marathon. That, too, would have been quite an accomplishment; but those who complete the half-marathon get a gold Donald Duck head for a medal, and I wanted Mickey Mouse. So it had to be the full 26.2 miles.

Our son gave me a book to follow, and my training began. I had to keep extending the miles, from 5, to 10, to 15, and then to 20.

I remember running 18 miles in the pouring rain and cold, and that's when I realized how badly I wanted that medal and how hard I was willing to work for it. That was the only thing that kept me going—the desire to accomplish that task and get that medal!

Finally, the big day was almost upon me; and when my husband Tom and I went to the Wide World of Sports complex to pick up my packet containing all the necessary things needed for the next morning, I kind of went numb. The thought hit me like a ton of bricks, "What in the world do you think you are doing?" Doubt, nervousness, and fear started setting in, because this was reality, and it was going to happen in just a matter of hours. Needless to say, I didn't sleep much that night; and the alarm rang at 3:00 a.m. The morning for which I had prepared for months was here.

It was still very dark at 4:00 a.m. when we had to be there. And it was only 26 degrees. That year Florida had one of its coldest winters. The wait was excruciating, but finally the announcer told all the "athletes" to gather at the starting position. Tom looked at this Grandma and said, "Did you ever think that YOU would be called an athlete?" We both had a big laugh. The serious and professional runners went first. And then at 6:10 a.m. the fireworks went up, Mickey Mouse appeared, and the race began. I had devised a system for me to follow. I knew that I wasn't going to be fast, but if I could keep my scheduled pace I would finish in the allowed time. Tom was at the five-mile marker cheering me on. When I got to the halfway point, friends of ours, who surprised me by being there, were right there with Tom to encourage me. That was such a huge help. At mile 18, I was really getting tired. It was still so cold that all the runners stayed stiff, and that's not a good way to run. And at every water station many fell, because when runners grabbed their water, they would drink it and then throw the cup. Well, in that cold, the excess water froze, and it became very slippery. So I slowed way down at water stations. I knew it would hurt my time, but I didn't want to fall and maybe hurt myself and then not be able to continue. At mile 23, I got a cramp in my leg. Sometimes when cramping starts, it doesn't stop and it's impossible to run. Of course, I thought, "I can't quit now. I've come too far." I kept going and tried my best to stretch my leg. I certainly wasn't the most graceful runner at that point, but I couldn't have cared less. The cramp finally subsided, and

I was thrilled to think that the qualifying time I needed to achieve in order to get that medal was now obtainable. There was a man along the final route who yelled my name and told me to watch for what was around the corner. There was a band playing, and then I saw it—two of the most beautiful words I have ever seen: FINISH LINE!

I was running strong, and the tears started to flow. I saw Tom and our friends jumping up and down! Tom started running with me along the fence. I crossed the line, and there stood a gentleman who looked at me, saw the tears running down my face, and of all the phrases he could have said to me, he said this: "Well done!" And then he put the gold Mickey Mouse medal around my neck. I got the medal! I got the medal! It was worth it all—every bit of the training and every ache and pain. I got the medal!

Yes, I am very glad that I ran that race. Our son had warned me that there would be moments during my training where I would be so mad at him for getting me into this, but then there would also be moments where I would be so glad that he had pushed me because I wouldn't have wanted to miss the feeling at the end. He was so right!

During the race, I couldn't help but recall Bible verses I had learned. The race seemed to give me a better understanding of their meaning. For instance, the verse where the apostle Paul tells us that we are not to look back, but press on and strain toward the goal to win the prize (Phil. 3:14). Life is like a marathon run. Studying God's Word is the refreshment we need in this life. Becoming Christ-like in our thoughts, words, and deeds is the prize we should be seeking. There are high points and low points; but if we have the STRONG desire to finish, we will, and we will hear Jesus say, "Welcome home." And hopefully He will add, "`Well done, good and faithful servant!`" (Matthew 25:21a.) He will then give us our "medal"—HEAVEN, where we will dwell with Him, and He with us.

If you want something bad enough, you will do whatever it takes to get it—but we must be careful to do it the right and honest way. You will push yourself beyond what you thought you could do to obtain that goal.

My prayer as you study this book, which will take you through much of the Old Testament, is that you will have a great and strong desire to learn about and want to know the purpose of the Old

Testament and not just put it away because you think it's not for you. This study is also like a marathon run in that there will be a lot of ground to cover. But it will be so worth your while if you <u>really</u> desire to understand God more and are willing to see how much God loves you. He proved that by what He was willing to go through to provide a Savior for you and the world—the ultimate MEDAL! There are signposts of Jesus everywhere in the Old Testament. It's all about Him. Let me help you to see that. It will be my privilege— for God is pleased and honored when His children desire to learn more about Him!

PROLOGUE

Maybe you have never thought about this before, so I am going to ask the question: Have you ever wondered when time actually started and if or when it is going to end? I can't say that it was ever of the utmost importance to me. Now, I would hear occasionally through a song or something I may have read, the phrase "when time shall be no more." It's a hard concept to grasp because we only know a life that is structured by time. We are constantly looking at our watches or cell phones to check the time. We live in a world where we think every second matters, and we all have places to go and people to see, and there is NEVER enough time. We are controlled by time. Well, you know what? That little phrase is true. There is coming a moment in our lives when "time" will be no more.

In my study of the Old Testament this past year, I had to sit and wait for answers and simple clarification from the discernment the Holy Spirit ✝ promises to provide. Let's face it. The Old Testament is quite a challenging study. During one of the times when I was sitting and waiting for understanding, I had a real sense of the Holy Spirit communicating directly with me. To me it was so profound that I caught myself jumping out of my seat. It excited me so, because what the Holy Spirit allowed me to grasp made perfect sense. There was a definite time in history when time as we understand it began, and there is going to be a definite time in the future when time as we know it will end. But we must not miss all that lies in between. Let me do my best to lay it out for you. From when time started to when it will end, there are seven "eras." According to Webster, another word for era is epoch, cycle, age, or time period.

Biblical time periods are divided into seven different eras:

1.   The Era of Creation and Perfection
        In Genesis 1:14-18 it clearly states:

> *And God said, "Let there be lights in the*
> *expanse of the sky to separate the day from*
> *the night, and let them serve as signs to*
> *mark seasons and days and years, and let*
> *them be lights in the expanse of the sky to*
> *give light on the earth." And it was so. God*
> *made two great lights—the greater light to*
> *govern the day and the lesser light to govern*
> *the night. He also made the stars. God set*
> *them in the expanse of the sky to give light*
> *on the earth, to govern the day and the*
> *night, and to separate light from darkness.*
> *And God saw that it was good.*

Once the universe started its rotation, time as we know it began. Oh, what an era that was! To tell you the truth, we cannot even begin to comprehend it. After everything God created, He announced that IT WAS GOOD.

And then from Genesis 1:26-31, we read that God created a man and a woman. Look closely at verses 26 and 31 and you will see the wonder of God's love for His children from the very beginning: 26a, *Then God said, "Let us make man in our image, in our likeness."* and 31a, *God saw all that he had made, and it was very good.* That's right. We were made in the image and likeness of God our creator. ✝ What a privilege, honor, and responsibility! And did you note in verse 31 that God judged His creation of man as not only good, but very good?

Adam and Eve were perfect. Their relationship with God and with each other was perfect. Can you get a grip on that one? God gave them a perfect Garden of Eden to live in. They were complete. They absolutely had everything they needed. There was no such thing as "want" because God had provided EVERYTHING that was needed to fulfill mankind. Imagine living a life of total contentment, satisfaction, and joy, and that is exactly how God intended it. That is why He created this world. It is for us to enjoy. But most of all, He created it so we could enjoy it with Him and bring Him the glory. That was the era of Creation and Perfection.

2.   The Era of the Fall of Man
          This Era changed everything. Would you please just take the time to read right now this devastating account from Genesis 3:1-13a? I tried to take some verses out to shorten it for you, but I couldn't. It is imperative that you grasp the magnitude of what happened that sad, sad day.

> *1Now the serpent was more crafty than any of the wild animals the* LORD *God had made. He said to the woman, "Did God really say, `You must not eat from any tree in the garden'?"*
>
> *2The woman said to the serpent, "We may eat fruit from the trees in the garden, 3but God did say, `You must not eat fruit from the tree that is in the middle of the garden, and you must not touch it, or you will die.' "*
>
> *4"You will not surely die," the serpent said to the woman. 5"For God knows that when you eat of it your eyes will be opened, and you will be like God, knowing good and evil."*
>
> *6When the woman saw that the fruit of the tree was good for food and pleasing to the eye, and also desirable for gaining wisdom, she took some and ate it. She also gave some to her husband, who was with her, and he ate it. 7Then the eyes of both of them were opened, and they realized they*

were naked; so they sewed fig leaves together and made coverings for themselves.

8Then the man and his wife heard the sound of the LORD God as he was walking in the garden in the cool of the day, and they hid from the LORD God among the trees of the garden. 9But the LORD God called to the man, "Where are you?"

10He answered, "I heard you in the garden, and I was afraid because I was naked; so I hid."

11And he said, "Who told you that you were naked? Have you eaten from the tree that I commanded you not to eat from?"

12The man said, "The woman you put here with me—she gave me some fruit from the tree, and I ate it."

13aThen the LORD God said to the woman, "What is this you have done?"

Man's first sin ✞ changed everything! It was just the beginning, because sin got uglier and uglier. In Genesis 4, we see the story of an angry Cain killing his brother Abel because of pride and jealousy. Think about that. Those thoughts, or words like shame, blame, embarrassment, etc. were non-existent in the era of creation and perfection.

Sin continued to permeate and spread like a cancer through society as a whole. For in Genesis 6, we read the story of Noah. There was only ONE man on the face of this earth who was living right before God. God had had enough, and He destroyed the earth by a flood, saving only Noah, his family (God extended His loving concern to the whole family of righteous Noah), and two of each living creature and animal.

And then in Genesis 11, we see another sad example of the sinful pride of mankind and how slow we are to learn from the experiences of the past. In an effort to make a name for "themselves," the descendants of the survivors of the flood erected the Tower of Babel. The Lord God was not impressed, and He confused their language and scattered them from there to all over the earth. The fall of man was the darkest era ever. Everything looked hopeless.

3.   The Era of the Promise
        This era takes us from Genesis 12 to the time of John the Baptist.   This is when you really start to see the unconditional love and grace of God.   He chose a certain man named Abram (Abraham), and by God using him a nation was born that would bring forth a Savior with salvation for sinful mankind. Read Genesis 12:2-3:

> *"I will make you into a great nation and I will bless you; I will make your name great, and you will be a blessing. I will bless those who bless you, and whoever curses you I will curse; and all peoples on earth will be blessed through you."*

Also read Genesis 17:3-8:

> *Abram fell facedown, and God said to him, "As for me, this is my covenant with you: You will be the father of many nations. No longer will you be called Abram; your name will be Abraham, for I have made you a father of many nations. I will make you very fruitful; I will make nations of you, and kings will come from you. I will establish my covenant as an everlasting covenant between me and you and your descendants after you for the generations to come, to be your God and the God of your descendants after you. The whole land of Canaan, where you are now an alien, I will give as an*

everlasting possession to you and your descendants after you; and I will be their God."

So, this era consisted of Abraham and his sons, whom we call the patriarchs. They were Abraham, Isaac, and Jacob. (Jacob's name was changed to Israel.) Theirs is a long but wonderful story. I would love it if you would just take the time to open that Bible of yours and read Genesis 12-50. It's better than any compelling novel. You will not want to put it down. (You are going to have to trust me on this one and just plain do it.) You won't be sorry. From those chapters you will see that when Jacob's family went to Egypt, there were about 70 of them. Many generations later, there were so many Israelites that the Pharaoh was nervous for fear of a takeover. So he made them slaves and tortured them. To deliver His chosen people out of Egypt, God brought onto the scene a man named Moses. Then came Joshua, the judges, the kings, the prophets, and finally John the Baptist. Other than John the Baptist, this era is covered in the Old Testament. THIS is where this book is going to have its focus—in the Era of the Promise. But I will list the rest of the eras of time.

4.   The Era of Salvation—the Era of Jesus
        If you study the four Gospels in the New Testament, you will better understand this era of time: the birth, life, death, resurrection, and ascension of the Christ. The more you study this era, the deeper your love for your Savior will grow. He certainly is the hope and mentor for us in how to experience the abundant life through faith in Him while we are living in this world. Why merely survive, when there is so much more to get up for every morning?

5.   The Era of the Holy Spirit and the Great Commission
        In Acts 1, Jesus told his disciples they were now to become apostles because they were going to be sent out to tell the gospel (the good news of Jesus and His love) to the

nations. What a glorious job—and what a responsibility! Jesus knew they did not have the power to accomplish that on their own, so He told them to go to Jerusalem and WAIT. In Acts 2, it is made very clear Who they had been waiting for. Jesus knew that every one of them (and us for that matter) needed Him to accomplish the job. He, in His human body, could not be all places at all times. So He sent His Spirit to empower them to do what no man can do on his own; that is, to be the hands, feet, and reflection of Jesus. The book of Acts does not have an ending because the job of telling this gospel to our families, to our neighbors, and to the nations is not done yet. Acts of spreading the gospel still have to keep happening. This is our time era, right here, right now. We are still a work in progress era—a present and ongoing one until Christ comes again.

6. The Era of Christ's Return

This era is described in Revelation 19-20. Christ returns on a white horse, and His Name is Faithful and True. It is in this era that the Battle of Armageddon is fought. It is where the antichrist and the false prophet are thrown alive into the fiery lake of burning sulfur. This is the era of Jesus' thousand year reign, when Satan will be bound and then released for a short season. But in verse 10 of chapter 20 we read:

> *And the devil, who deceived them, was thrown into the lake of burning sulfur, where the beast and the false prophet had been thrown. They will be tormented day and night for ever and ever.*

After that comes the Judgment. Verse 15 says, *If anyone's name was not found written in the book of life, he was thrown into the lake of fire.* This earth as we know it will be no more. Evil will be banished to eternal hell.

7.   The Era of the New Heaven and New Earth
          In Revelation 21:3b-6a, John writes that he saw a
new heaven and a new earth, for the first heaven and the first
earth had passed away. And now, friends, this is where the
structure of time will be NO MORE.

> *"Now the dwelling of God is with men, and
> he will live with them. They will be his
> people, and God himself will be with them
> and be their God. He will wipe every tear
> from their eyes. There will be no more death
> or mourning or crying or pain, for the old
> order of things has passed away."*
>
> *He who was seated on the throne
> said, "I am making everything new!" Then
> he said, "Write this down, for these words
> are trustworthy and true."*
>
> *He said to me: "It is done. I am the
> Alpha and the Omega, the Beginning and
> the End."*

          He had the power to begin time ✞, and He did in
Genesis 1. And He most certainly has the power to end time,
which He will do as described in Revelation 21.

          One might wonder how best to study the Old Testament. It
is kind of like the study of the book of Revelation. Some are afraid
of it. Some do not like or understand all the killing in the Old
Testament. And it's old. That is why it is called the Old Testament;
and many of us think we should always be moving forward, never
looking back. We think we should be more contemporary and
progressive and that the Old Testament can't possibly be relevant
anymore. We often say, "Let's get into the New Testament, because
it's all about Jesus now anyway, right? What good is all that old
stuff?"
          Those were my thoughts (in my ignorance) for too long. I
discovered what a committed and serious study with dedicated time

spent in His Word under the power of His Holy Spirit will do! It literally transformed my way of thinking. (The Holy Spirit can do that for you, too!) I just can't say thank you enough to the Holy Spirit. Oh, where I would still be! It chills me to even think about it. I've got to tell you, I have changed my tune. I am singing a new song because the Old Testament IS, and I am going to say it again, the Old Testament IS all about Jesus! I have discovered that the whole Old Testament reveals how our gracious Father—who did not have to—loved us so much. He knew a Savior was the ONLY way to buy us back (redeem us) and bridge the gigantic gulf sin created between us and Him. And do you know what? IT WORKED!

But it did not just happen one Christmas morning. There had to have been a heart to heart agreement between the Father and His Son on what would be required of God the Son to become mankind's Savior to the satisfaction of God the Father. Then there was the LOOOONG process to get Jesus into that manger in Bethlehem. That took awhile (according to God's perfect timing), and the details are captured in the Old Testament—a testament of how God chose to work with and through humans to accomplish His plan of Redemption for you and me. And because of God's choice, mankind was blessed to have Him work through them. So, from the promise of a Savior in Genesis, to John the Baptist, God got the job done! I get it now! This is the way God chose to give us a future Savior and give us the good news found in the New Testament—all beginning with the timeline found in the Old Testament. There is no way we can fully appreciate God's love, grace, and patience until we study the Old Testament. In either the Old or New Testament, Jesus is the central figure. (The Old and New Testament fit together like a perfectly fitting glove on "your" hand.)

To provide Biblical support for the "Mysterious" portion of my book title, let me share these Bible passages [emphasis mine]:

> Romans 16:25, *Now to him who is able to establish you by my gospel and the proclamation of Jesus Christ, according to the revelation of the _mystery_ hidden for long ages past,*

Colossians 1:25-26, *I have become its servant by the commission God gave me to present to you the word of God in its fullness--the mystery that has been kept hidden for ages and generations, but is now disclosed to the saints.*

Colossians 2:2-3, *My purpose is that they may be encouraged in heart and united in love, so that they may have the full riches of complete understanding, in order that they may know the mystery of God, namely, Christ, in whom are hidden all the treasures of wisdom and knowledge.*

Ephesians 1:9-10, *And he made known to us the mystery of his will according to his good pleasure, which he purposed in Christ, to be put into effect when the times will have reached their fulfillment--to bring all things in heaven and on earth together under one head, even Christ.*

At the end of this prologue, and of each chapter, you will find a Jesus signpost recap. A page reference will be given where you will find this sign ✞ representing a Jesus signpost. I hope you will find it helpful in discovering Jesus' footsteps in our study of the Old Testament. For you see, whether the Old or New Testament, your salvation or condemnation, you too will discover: It's all about Jesus!

I dare you to come with me on this Old Testament journey and discover that the greatest treasure found in the treasure chest of God's greatness and faithfulness is His precious Son, Jesus.

PROLOGUE

JESUS'  SIGNPOSTS

"Holy Spirit": ✞ Pg. 15

● ...John 15:26, *"When the Counselor comes, whom I* [Jesus] *will send to you from the Father, the Spirit of truth who goes out from the Father, he will testify about me."*

● ...John 14:25-26, *"All this I* [Jesus] *have spoken while still with you. But the Counselor, the Holy Spirit, whom the Father will send in my name, will teach you all things and will remind you of everything I have said to you."*

"God our Creator" (Jesus): ✞ Pg. 16

● ...John 1:3, *Through him* [Jesus] *all things were made; without him nothing was made that has been made.*

● ...Colossians 1:15-16, *He* [Jesus] *is the image of the invisible God, the firstborn over all creation. For by him all things were created: things in heaven and on earth, visible and invisible, whether thrones or powers or rulers or authorities; all things were created by him and for him.*

● ...Romans 11:36, *For from him* [Jesus] *and through him* [Jesus] *and to him are all things. To him be the glory forever! Amen*

"First Sin": ✛ Pg. 18

Now a Savior would be needed to shed blood and die to provide a Righteous covering for mankind's sin and allow man to live forever with God.

● …Genesis 3:21-24, *The LORD God **made garments of skin for Adam and his wife and clothed them.** And the LORD God said, "The man has now become like one of us, knowing good and evil. **He must not be allowed to reach out his hand and take also from the tree of life and eat, and live forever."** So the LORD God banished him from the Garden of Eden to work the ground from which he had been taken. After he drove the man out, he placed on the east side of the Garden of Eden cherubim and a flaming sword flashing back and forth to guard the way to the tree of life.*

● …John 19:33-34, *But when they came to **Jesus and found that he was already dead,** they did not break his legs. Instead, one of the **soldiers pierced Jesus' side with a spear, bringing a sudden flow of blood and water.***

● …2 Corinthians 6:21, *God made **him who had no sin** [Jesus] to be sin for us, **so that in him we might become the righteousness of God.***

● …Matthew 28:5-7, *The angel said to the women, "Do not be afraid, for I know that you are looking for Jesus, who was crucified. He is not here; he has risen, just as he said. Come and see the place where he lay. **Then go quickly and tell his disciples: `He has risen from the dead** and is going ahead of you into Galilee. There you will see him.' Now I have told you."*

● …John 11:25-26, ***Jesus said to her, "I am the resurrection and the life. He who believes in me will live, even though he*** *dies; and whoever lives and believes in me will never die. Do you believe this?"*

"Begin Time": ✞ Pg. 22

●...Genesis 1:1, *In the beginning God created the heavens and the earth.*

●...John 1:1-2 (GW), *In the beginning the Word* [Jesus] **already existed**. *The Word* [Jesus] *was with God, and the Word* [Jesus] *was God. He* [Jesus] *was **already with God** in the beginning.*

●...John 8:57-58, *"You are not yet fifty years old," the Jews said to him* [Jesus], *"and you have seen Abraham!" "I tell you the truth," Jesus answered, "before Abraham was born, I am!"*

●...Romans 9:5, *Theirs are the patriarchs, and from them is traced the human ancestry of Christ, who is God over all, forever praised! Amen.*

*Underline, bold, bracket inserts, additional emphasis mine.

1

THE PROMISE

When God gave "the Promise" to Abraham, the thought went through my mind, "Why him?" Why did God choose Abraham and then eventually the Jewish nation to bring the Messiah to the world? When you look at and study his history and family tree in Genesis 11, something extraordinary jumps out at you. We read in Joshua 24:2:

> *Joshua said to all the people, "This is what the LORD, the God of Israel, says: 'Long ago your forefathers, including Terah the father of Abraham and Nahor, lived beyond the River and worshiped other gods.'"* [Perhaps he was a moon god worshiper.] *Insert mine.

How incredible that despite Abraham's upbringing under the influence of a father who practiced idolatry, God chose Abraham. What was God thinking? Don't be fooled—God can convert any hearts in spite of their pasts or family influences to accomplish His purposes through their lives. That should be of great comfort to you, either for your heart condition or the heart condition of someone you love. Remember: *Jesus looked at them and said, "With man this is impossible, but with God all things are possible"* (Matthew 19:26).

May I just stop here a minute and relate that to you and me? How often have you wondered why God chose you for a certain ministry, or maybe even a very difficult walk in life? Have you had a few questions that you would just love to ask Him point blank given the chance? Sometimes as you get older, you take the opportunity to look back, and you are able to "see" that His hand was leading you in a direction you might never have gone. And then you marvel at how He just knew what was right for you. But then maybe you are still living day-by-day in the middle of your question. Don't forget another "gift" Jesus provided for you. With Him as your Lord and Savior, you have been granted the privilege of approaching the holy throne of God the Father in prayer ✟ in His Son's name. Don't hesitate to take the opportunity to have a one-on-one audience with the King of kings.

It seems like at every corner in my ongoing walk through this life, I ask the Lord the same question: "Why did You pick me?"..."Why did You pick me to sing on Children's Bible Hour?" "Why did You pick me to be the last one chosen for teams day after day in school?" "Why was I chosen in my teen years to sing with a group from Youth for Christ?" "Why did a boyfriend break my heart?" "Why did I have a wayward child?" "Why were there difficult times in my marriage?" "Why did You give me a ministry of music, writing, speaking, and teaching?" See what I mean? Sometimes we see the answers as we grow physically and spiritually. But I think that the real answer, as with Abraham, is that God sees our hearts and what He can do through our lives. You see, He's the Sovereign One. That simply means that He's God and we are NOT. He knows that left to ourselves, His purpose for our creation would not be accomplished.

I experience true fulfillment in my life when I desire God's will for my life, search for it, find it, and then DO it. I'll tell you right now that if I had given in to my human hurt feelings when I heard someone tell me that they hated my guts, or that a certain lady would not come to a Bible Study that I taught because she didn't like me, I would have packed up and quit God's calling for my life many times. When we are verbally punched in the stomach, our first tendency is to quit.

Oh, I almost forgot one: a lady told me that I was a disgrace to the name of Jesus because I wore fingernail polish and I was fashionably dressed. It was at that service that a man, dressed in leather and chains, was just riding by the church. He saw the sign announcing our concert, came in, and after the concert gave his heart to the Lord. Didn't that lady see that? Let me tell you, I walked away that night thinking that SHE was a crabby looking woman with a rotten, legalistic attitude that can test a person's spirit and grieve the

Holy Spirit.   (But then I remembered what God said about forgiveness.)

> *"For if you forgive men when they sin against you,*
> *your heavenly Father will also forgive you. But if*
> *you do not forgive men their sins, your Father will*
> *not forgive your sins"* (Matthew 6:14-15).

On the way home that night, I have to admit, I started to doubt. Maybe she was right. Maybe I should quit. Maybe I have been wrong all this time. NO! GET AWAY FROM ME SATAN! People can affect your feelings, and that is why I repeat what I said before: true fulfillment is when you desire God's will for your life, search for it, find it, and then DO it. Sadly, I have to be reminded, and I will take this opportunity to remind you of Jesus and His experiences and example for you and me to get our servants' hearts to more closely resemble His. Read with me and be humbled:

From John 15:18-20a:

> *"If the world hates you, keep in mind that it hated*
> *me first. If you belonged to the world, it would love*
> *you as its own. As it is, you do not belong to the*
> *world, but I have chosen you out of the world. That*
> *is why the world hates you. Remember the words I*
> *spoke to you: `No servant is greater than his*
> *master.'"*

From Isaiah 53:

> *1 Who has believed our message*
> > *and to whom has the arm of the LORD been*
> > *revealed?*
> *2 He grew up before him like a tender shoot,*
> > *and like a root out of dry ground.*
> > *He had no beauty or majesty to attract us to him,*
> > *nothing in his appearance that we should*
> > *desire him.*

3He was despised and rejected by men,
>   a man of sorrows, and familiar with
suffering.
>   Like one from whom men hide their faces
>   >   he was despised, and we esteemed him not.
4Surely he took up our infirmities
>   and carried our sorrows,
>   yet we considered him stricken by God,
>   smitten by him, and afflicted.
5But he was pierced for our transgressions,
>   he was crushed for our iniquities;
>   the punishment that brought us peace was upon him,
>   and by his wounds we are healed.
6We all, like sheep, have gone astray,
>   each of us has turned to his own way;
>   and the LORD has laid on him
>   the iniquity of us all.
7He was oppressed and afflicted,
>   yet he did not open his mouth;
>   he was led like a lamb to the slaughter
>   and as a sheep before her shearers is silent,
>   so he did not open his mouth.
8By oppression and judgment he was taken away.
>   And who can speak of his descendants?
>   For he was cut off from the land of the living;
>   for the transgression of my people he was
>   stricken.
9He was assigned a grave with the wicked,
>   and with the rich in his death,
>   though he had done no violence,
>   nor was any deceit in his mouth.
10Yet it was the LORD's will to crush him and cause
him to suffer,
>   and though the LORD makes his life a guilt
>   offering,
>   he will see his offspring and prolong his days,

*and the will of the LORD will prosper in his
hand.*

*11 After the suffering of his soul,
he will see the light of life and be satisfied;
by his knowledge my righteous servant will
justify many,
and he will bear their iniquities.*

*12 Therefore I will give him a portion among the
great,
and he will divide the spoils with the strong,
because he poured out his life unto death,
and was numbered with the transgressors.
For he bore the sin of many,
and made intercession for the transgressors.*

From Mark 14:34-36:

*"My soul is overwhelmed with sorrow to the point of
death," he said to them. "Stay here and keep watch."
Going a little farther, he fell to the ground and
prayed that if possible the hour might pass from him.
"Abba, Father," he said, "everything is possible for
you. Take this cup from me. Yet not what I will, but
what you will."*

If we emulate that kind of heartfelt lifestyle, when we go to
bed at night and when we are at the end of our lives, we will know
that we have made a difference for the Kingdom of God. Praise the
Lord! If you ask me, that's real livin'. But I guess that's up to you
and whether or not that is your goal in life. Thank goodness, it
became Abraham's!

For reasons only God knows, Abraham accepted the call.
God said to him in Genesis 12:1, *"Leave your country, your people
and your father's household and go to the land I will show you."*

That's pretty much God telling Abraham to leave everything
that is secure and comfortable to him—just leave, and God would
provide more information as needed. That is a powerful example of
step-by-step walking by faith in God, my friend. The Lord was

going to teach Abraham that life doesn't have to be (and most of the time may not be) comfortable in His will. But Abraham would find that he could find complete security in his God if he just trusted Him. I do believe that is a lesson or principle the Lord is still trying to get through to our hard, human heads yet today. In verse 4 we read, *So Abram left, as the LORD had told him....*

Simple obedience. You know, I will be saying this in some form at least a hundred times in the course of this book, so you'd better get used to it: God's instructions are NOT hard to understand. He hasn't changed. It is simple: obedience reaps blessings; disobedience reaps consequences. Now come on, does it take a rocket scientist to get that? I would say not. You will see proof of that simple statement in the lives of every human being we study. We should have learned that lesson by now. It truly shows us that our selfish and prideful self-will is inferior to God's perfect and pleasing will for our lives, and that is something the Lord WILL break us of some time, some way. Mark my words.

The battle of our human nature wanting to be in control, instead of "Let Go and Let God," is something every one of us has to fight. The apostle Paul in Ephesians 6:10-18 illustrates that for us and shows us what it takes to fight that battle, too:

> *Finally, be strong in the Lord and in his mighty power. Put on the full armor of God so that you can take your stand against the devil's schemes. For our struggle is not against flesh and blood, but against the rulers, against the authorities, against the powers of this dark world and against the spiritual forces of evil in the heavenly realms. Therefore put on the full armor of God, so that when the day of evil comes, you may be able to stand your ground, and after you have done everything, to stand. Stand firm then, with the belt of truth buckled around your waist, with the breastplate of righteousness in place, and with your feet fitted with the readiness that comes from the gospel of peace. In addition to all this, take up the shield of faith, with which you can extinguish all the flaming arrows of the evil one.*

Take the helmet of salvation and the sword of the
Spirit, which is the word of God. And pray in the
Spirit on all occasions with all kinds of prayers and
requests. With this in mind, be alert and always keep
on praying for all the saints.

Take note how Paul says that we have to "put on" the full
armor. That's like dressing every morning. We figure out the plan
for the day, the weather, and then we determine what attire will fit
both. We make that choice, and then we make the effort to put it on.
The same goes for the full armor described in this passage. We must
understand that we will be fighting the enemy of our soul all day, and
he will desperately try to get our eyes fixed on ourselves rather than
on Jesus. Then we will make the choice whether or not to put on the
right clothing (armor) to meet the day head on—totally prepared for
whatever comes our way.

The story of Abraham is found in Genesis 12-25. You will
see that he certainly was no different than any one of us. There were
days that he chose to put on the "full armor of God" and then there
were days he did not. I am here to tell you, the difference is
UNBELIEVABLE! One of his greatest faith-testing moments was
when his will and faith were SO in tune with his God. (That story is
found in Genesis 22.) You and I have to stand back and say that we
could never have done what he did. You see, Abraham and his wife
Sarah were past the years of child-bearing, and yet God promised
Abraham that his descendents would be as numerous as the sands on
the seashore and the stars in the sky. They waited and waited, and
during their wait, Sarah grew impatient and tried to help God out.
(Isn't that hilarious? And yet, we, too, do it all the time. Oh, but
haven't we all done some foolhardy things in our lives?). Sarah,
seeing that she was barren, told her husband to go and be with her
servant girl, and then his seed could still fulfill God's promise. You
must read that story in Genesis 16.

Step out of God's will and there WILL be consequences, and
there were. But just when you have the overwhelming feeling that
all is hopeless, remember that God has a purpose for His timing. Oh
yes, that is a REALLY good life lesson. In Genesis 21, just like He
promised (when are we going to learn that we serve a God who

ALWAYS keeps His promises?), this couple miraculously had a son—Isaac. How precious that child must have been to them. That was the child that God had promised, and He had huge plans for Isaac.

But, let's get back to Genesis 22 where Abraham's faith was being tested to the max. Listen to these words:

1Some time later God tested Abraham. He said to him, "Abraham!"

"Here I am," he replied.

2Then God said, "Take your son, your only son, Isaac, whom you love, and go to the region of Moriah. Sacrifice him there as a burnt offering on one of the mountains I will tell you about."

3Early the next morning Abraham got up and saddled his donkey. He took with him two of his servants and his son Isaac. When he had cut enough wood for the burnt offering, he set out for the place God had told him about. 4On the third day Abraham looked up and saw the place in the distance. 5He said to his servants, "Stay here with the donkey while I and the boy go over there. We will worship and then we will come back to you."

6Abraham took the wood for the burnt offering and placed it on his son Isaac, and he himself carried the fire and the knife. As the two of them went on together, 7Isaac spoke up and said to his father Abraham, "Father?"

"Yes, my son?" Abraham replied.

"The fire and wood are here," Isaac said, "but where is the lamb for the burnt offering?"

8Abraham answered, "God himself will provide the lamb for the burnt offering, my son." And the two of them went on together. ✝

9When they reached the place God had told him about, Abraham built an altar there and arranged the wood on it. He bound his son Isaac and laid him on the altar, on top of the wood.

10Then he reached out his hand and took the knife to slay his son. 11But the angel of the LORD called out to him from heaven, "Abraham! Abraham!"

"Here I am," he replied.

12"Do not lay a hand on the boy," he said. "Do not do anything to him. Now I know that you fear God, because you have not withheld from me your son, your only son."

13Abraham looked up and there in a thicket he saw a ram caught by its horns. He went over and took the ram and sacrificed it as a burnt offering instead of his son. 14So Abraham called that place The LORD Will Provide. And to this day it is said, "On the mountain of the LORD it will be provided."

15The angel of the LORD called to Abraham from heaven a second time 16and said, "I swear by myself, declares the LORD, that because you have done this and have not withheld your son, your only son, 17I will surely bless you and make your descendants as numerous as the stars in the sky and as the sand on the seashore. Your descendants will take possession of the cities of their enemies, 18and through your offspring all nations on earth will be blessed, because you have obeyed me" (Genesis 22:1-18).

All I can say is WOW! How did Abraham do that? I know how he did it. He believed the Lord's promise to him. Yes, it is that simple. If we would just believe God's promises to us, it would radically change our lives. Faith is the centerpiece of our walk with the Lord. The question we should always ask ourselves as a gauge of our faith is, "Do I really believe with all my heart the promises of God?" Doubt is the main culprit when it comes to destroying our faith. Satan used it in Genesis 3 with Eve, and he still uses it with us today. Let Abraham be an example to us of what is possible when our faith is strong. Faith pleases God (Hebrews 11:6), and Jesus said in Matthew 17:20b-21:

> *"I tell you the truth, if you have faith as small as a mustard seed, you can say to this mountain, 'Move from here to there' and it will move. Nothing will be impossible for you."*

Do you have any "mountain" (challenge) in your life that needs to be moved? Exercise your faith. Look at the "mountain" that Abraham needed moved. There is your proof.

Don't be swept away in our study of Abraham to be fooled into thinking he was a <u>perfect</u> man. (Make no mistake—<u>only</u> Jesus was, is, and forever will be perfect.) To illustrate this, let's look at Abraham's action in Genesis 12:11-13:

> *As he was about to enter Egypt, he said to his wife Sarai, "I know what a beautiful woman you are. When the Egyptians see you, they will say, 'This is his wife.' Then they will kill me but will let you live. Say you are my sister, so that I will be treated well for your sake and my life will be spared because of you."*

And in sinful irony, we see a "like father, like son" illustration of Adam's sin seed continuing its progression down through the ages. Here, from Abraham to Isaac. See Genesis 26:7:

> *When the men of that place asked him [Isaac] about his wife, he said, "She is my sister," because he was afraid to say, "She is my wife." He thought, "The men of this place might kill me on account of Rebekah, because she is beautiful."*

There it is—two perfect examples of what we looked at earlier in this chapter. Remember our discussion on the "armor" of God? Do you think Abraham and Isaac looked to God in faith during that "mountain" experience? Or, do you think they fell for Satan's subtle plot that got them to look to "self" for the solution?

Feelings get bigger than faith when YOU think instead of asking God what HE thinks. Also, like Sarah, Rebekah was barren. But, in this case, Isaac learned from his father's mistake and waited and prayed on behalf of his wife. The Lord answered that prayer with a hardy YES by giving them twin sons, Jacob and Esau; but despite being twins, they could not have been more different in looks and in temperament. Unfortunately, Isaac and Rebekah picked favorites. Because the firstborn was to get the birthright and the father's blessing (and Esau was born first), Rebekah connived and deceived to make sure that Jacob got it (Genesis 27). This was one dysfunctional family! (See, you aren't the only one with family difficulties after all. It is nothing new.) It's no wonder that family had drifted so far away from the Lord. They were all concerned about themselves, and again I say that is a root problem, always— when we disconnect from God and depend on our own way of thinking. This family was a mess, and Esau couldn't wait to get his hands on his brother to kill him for stealing his birthright. Jacob ran for his life, and just when he thought all was hopeless, God stepped in. Read this: Genesis 28:10-19a:

> *10Jacob left Beersheba and set out for Haran. 11When he reached a certain place, he stopped for the night because the sun had set. Taking one of the stones there, he put it under his head and lay down to sleep. 12He had a dream in which he saw a stairway resting on the earth, with its top reaching to heaven, and the angels of God were ascending and descending on it. 13There above it stood the LORD, and he said: "I am the LORD, the God of your father Abraham and the God of Isaac. I will give you and your descendants the land on which you are lying. 14Your descendants will be like the dust of the earth, and you will spread out to the west and to the east, to the north and to the south. All peoples on earth will be blessed through you and your offspring. 15I am with you and will watch over you wherever you go,*

and I will bring you back to this land. I will not leave you until I have done what I have promised you."

16When Jacob awoke from his sleep, he thought, "Surely the LORD is in this place, and I was not aware of it." 17He was afraid and said, "How awesome is this place! This is none other than the house of God; this is the gate of heaven."

18Early the next morning Jacob took the stone he had placed under his head and set it up as a pillar and poured oil on top of it. 19He called that place Bethel.

The Lord knew that Jacob needed this crisis to feel helplessness, and as a result Jacob found HIS God—not his father's, or even his grandfather's, but HIS. Remember, God does not have grandchildren. Everyone needs a Bethel experience. ✝ When you realize that being a Christian (choosing to follow Christ) cannot be handed down in a will but has to be personal action—VERY personal—you will then find that your life will never be the same. God always knows just what we need and when we need it. Naturally, God had plans for Jacob.

The Lord led Jacob to the house of Laban. He fell in love with Laban's daughter Rachel and was willing to work seven long years for the right to marry her. At the end of the seven years, Laban deceived Jacob by giving him his other daughter, Leah. Jacob worked another seven years to get his beloved Rachel, but then one has to wonder if Jacob sensed "What goes around comes around." Do you think Jacob then had a better understanding of how hurtful deception is and its lasting consequences? He became a man of great wealth working for his father-in-law, and that became a thorn of dissention. So Jacob secretly fled from Laban, taking all of his flocks and family with him. Laban came after him, but with the Lord's help, they worked it all out. Jacob knew that he now had to go back and face the music, so to speak, with Esau. You see, salvation (that Bethel experience) is the most important event in our lives. But to live abundantly in the way the Lord intended, He demands that we give our ALL. Oh, don't we wish that the song, "I Surrender All" was instead, "I Surrender Part of it All," and that would be sufficient. But it isn't. Again, I say, He demands our all. This next event in Jacob's life is what completed Jacob and will complete us too; and yet, other than repentance, it is the hardest to do. It goes completely against our human nature. Read what must happen to Jacob before he faces Esau in Genesis 32:22-31:

> *22That night Jacob got up and took his two wives, his two maidservants and his eleven sons and crossed the ford of the Jabbok. 23After he had sent them across the stream, he sent over all his possessions. 24So Jacob was left alone, and a man wrestled with him till daybreak. 25When the man saw that he could not overpower him, he touched the socket of Jacob's hip so that his hip was wrenched as he wrestled with the man. 26Then the man said, "Let me go, for it is daybreak."*
>
> *But Jacob replied, "I will not let you go unless you bless me."*
>
> *27The man asked him, "What is your name?"*
>
> *"Jacob," he answered.*
>
> *28Then the man said, "Your name will no longer be Jacob, but Israel, because you have struggled with God and with men and have overcome."*
>
> *29Jacob said, "Please tell me your name."*
>
> *But he replied, "Why do you ask my name?" Then he blessed him there.*
>
> *30So Jacob called the place Peniel, saying, "It is because I saw God face to face, and yet my life was spared."*
>
> *31The sun rose above him as he passed Peniel, and he was limping because of his hip.*

I told you that the Lord had plans for Jacob. But the breaking down of our stubborn, strong, self-will is no easy task, is it?

But that is what surrender means. Again (and I am not ashamed to repeat it), it is what the Lord demands.

Jacob had many sons, and unfortunately again, like father, like son, he picked a favorite—Joseph. Because of this, his brothers hated Joseph and sold him to Midianite merchants when their caravan passed by. They, in turn, took Joseph to Egypt and sold him to Potiphar, who was the captain of the guard for Pharaoh. The brothers told their father that Joseph had been killed by a wild animal, and Jacob was devastated to say the least. This story unfolds in Genesis 37-50. Later, because of a famine in the land, Jacob sent his sons to Egypt for grain. By this time, through many, many challenges (the Lord's master plan in motion), Joseph had become second in command to the Pharaoh himself. When the brothers were brought before Joseph, they had no idea it was Joseph. Joseph recognized them, however. What would have been your natural response to someone who had hurt you so badly? Bitterness? Revenge? Those are just a couple responses that come quickly to mind. Can you imagine how scared to death those brothers were when Joseph revealed himself to them? I am sure they thought their days were numbered. Read what Joseph said to them in Genesis 50:20, *"You intended to harm me, but God intended it for good to accomplish what is now being done, the saving of many lives."*

Well, what do you think of that? That reminds me of a time when I was doing a lot of recording at a certain studio. When you pay to have song tracks made especially for you, they are yours. No one else may use them unless they are given permission. One day, I heard an introduction on the radio of one of my sound tracks, and then waited to hear my voice start to sing. But, instead, I heard someone else's. An artist knows his or her own track. I was stunned and quickly called my producer, who did not have an answer. That told me everything I needed to hear. I knew that from then on I could not go back to that producer again. I didn't want any trouble; I just knew I had to move on.

Within two weeks (out of the blue of heaven—thank You, Lord!), a producer from Iowa called and invited me to come down there and try out his studio and meet a very creative man on his staff. At that point Tom and I had nothing to lose, so we went. It was this producer and new-found friend that led me into a children's ministry for the next twenty-five years. That actually became a big part of our ministry that I became known for. In fact, one of the songs I did for years and years with children was called, "I'm God's Kid."

Awhile back, I was getting gas in my car, and a young man in his early twenties asked me if I was Lynnelle Pierce. I told him that I was. He went on to say that his mom made him come to all my concerts. He had this cute smile on his face to kind of show me that he hadn't really minded, he just didn't want his mom to know that. I reached up and patted him on his muscled shoulder and said thanks, and then he left. All of a sudden I noticed he had come back into the station, and he came back to me to say, "And I am STILL God's Kid." Words can't express how wonderful I felt. Then I thanked the Lord for changing our course of direction, and the way it started was through another's deception. What man does for his own selfish gain, God has a way of turning it all out for good. He does know what He's doing, and His plans are perfect. Case closed!

Joseph told his brothers to get their father and all their belongings and move to Egypt so he could take care of the whole bunch. The Israelites at that time were 70 in number and they multiplied in the land of Egypt. They were divided into 12 tribes because Jacob (Israel) had 12 sons. Later, we see that Joseph's two son's, Ephraim and Manasseh, become two tribes instead of Joseph, and Levi is not included in the 12 tribes because his family line became the priests of the Israelite nation—still leaving 12 tribes. You will see later in the book how the Lord used these tribes in His plan of sending Jesus here—especially the tribe of Judah.

I end this chapter with Exodus 1:6, *Now Joseph and all his brothers and all that generation died.*

Thus ends the era of Abraham and his immediate family. Let's read now how God moves His dear children along down His perfectly prepared path that eventually leads to His Son.

CHAPTER 1

JESUS' SIGNPOSTS

"Father in Prayer": ✞ Pg. 32

● ...Matthew 27:50-51, *And when Jesus had cried out again in a loud voice, he gave up his spirit. At that moment the curtain of the temple was torn in two from top to bottom.*

● ...Hebrews 10:19-20, *Therefore, brothers, since we have confidence to enter the Most Holy Place by the blood of Jesus, by a new and living way opened for us through the curtain, that is, his body,*

● ...John 15:16, *You did not choose me, but I chose you and appointed you to go and bear fruit--fruit that will last. Then the Father will give you whatever you ask in my name.*

"God Himself Will Provide the Lamb": ✞ Pg. 38

● ...John 1:29, *The next day John saw Jesus coming toward him and said, "Look, the Lamb of God, who takes away the sin of the world!*

●...1 Corinthians 5:7, *For Christ, our Passover lamb, has been sacrificed.*

●...1 Peter 1:19, *but with the precious blood of Christ, a lamb without blemish or defect.*

"Bethel Experience": ✟ Pg. 42

●...John 3:3, *In reply Jesus declared, "I tell you the truth, no one can see the kingdom of God unless he is born again."*

●...John 3:14b-15, *so the Son of Man must be lifted up, that everyone who believes in him may have eternal life.*

Lesson 1: The Promise
Passages from Genesis 3 - 50

1. Why do you need a Savior anyway? (Gen. 3)

2. Of all the nations in the world, what nation did God choose to bring Jesus, the Savior from? How did it all begin? (Gen. 12: 1-9.) What was Abram's response?

3. Have you ever had a call from God? What did He ask of you? What was YOUR response? Why is it so hard to obey His call? What must you "put on" every day? (Ephesians 6: 10-18.)

4. What was God's promise to Abram? (Gen. 15.) Abram had a few questions and doubts. What did he do with them? What can you learn from Abram?

5. What happened when Abram and Sarai jumped ahead of God's plan? (Gen. 16.) What were the results? Can you think of a time that you jumped ahead of God's plan? What were the results? When you move ahead of God, what does that really say about your faith in God?

6. What tested Abraham's faith the most? (Genesis 22.) Has God ever tested you? Why do you think He does that?

7. Abraham's family continues. Who were Isaac's sons? Give a short summary of what happened between these two boys. (Gen. 25:19-34 and Gen. 27.)

8. What happened to Jacob in Gen. 28 and then what happened to him in Gen. 32? Can you explain what those experiences meant in his spiritual life? Can you pinpoint a time when

those experiences happened to you? Why are they both necessary along your spiritual journey?

9.   Who was Joseph? Describe him. (Gen. 37) What was his life like? (Gen. 39 – 41.)

10.   What was Joseph's response to his brothers after all that they had done to him? (Gen.50.) What will an unforgiving spirit do to a relationship? What will forgiveness do to one? Is there someone you need to forgive despite what they have done to you?

11.   What was Jacob's name changed to? (Gen. 35:10.)

12.   Who were the twelve tribes of Israel that would become a great nation and God's chosen people? (Deuteronomy 33.)

2

God Prepares His Man
for the Job

As God's promise continues to unfold, we now move into the book of Exodus where we note in chapter 1:8, *Then a new king, who did not know about Joseph, came to power in Egypt.* Apparently, down through the generations, the story of Joseph and Jacob's little tribe of seventy, who came into Egypt during the years of the famine, did not get passed down. All this Pharaoh saw was that a group of outsiders named the Israelites had become much too numerous; and naturally, to him that meant a threat of a takeover one day. He came up with a plan in verse 10: *"Come, we must deal shrewdly with them or they will become even more numerous and, if war breaks out, will join our enemies, fight against us and leave the country."*

Always thinking the negative! Always feeling like someone is going to get one over on you. Doesn't that sound a little like a part of human nature that hasn't changed to this day? Over and over you will see in the course of the whole Old Testament that when "self importance" (you know, "It's all about me") was born in Genesis 3 (one of the deadliest results of sin, in my opinion), it affected and still affects mankind in the most severe way. It's like we have to keep one eye looking over our shoulder at all times because we think someone is going to stab us along the way. Isn't that a sad way to live—living in fear that someone is out to get you, hurt you, or destroy you in some way? That life of fear is found in businesses, churches, and families, and for that matter, any place a human is involved. And you know, once you have been "burned" by someone and your trust has taken a mortal wound, it becomes one hard wound to heal. And in the meantime, you live a life of utter cautiousness and fear of ever trusting another person again. Do you realize how awful that is? All meaningful relationships in every shape and form depend on trust. It's the foundation—the solid base that you feel you can stand on. When that turns to muck, or sinking sand, what have you got? You're watching your every step. God never intended for us to live like that. Already I am looking back at Era One and the perfection of the world at that time where those feelings were never heard of or even thought about. There are going to be so many times (in this book and as you live your life today) that you will see all that has changed in this world since sin reared its ugly head so long ago. Consider these two passages that support the impact sin has had on the human condition: Jeremiah 9:4-5:

> *"Beware of your friends;*
> > *do not trust your brothers.*
> *For every brother is a deceiver,*
> > *and every friend a slanderer.*
> *Friend deceives friend,*
> > *and no one speaks the truth.*
> *They have taught their tongues to lie;*
> > *they weary themselves with sinning.*

and John 2:23-25:

> *Now while he was in Jerusalem at the Passover Feast, many people saw the miraculous signs he was doing and believed in his name. But Jesus would not entrust himself to them, for he knew all men. He did not need man's testimony about man, for he knew what was in a man.*

In his fear, Pharaoh had to come up with a solution fast! He was a pagan and a worshiper of many gods, but you can see he really didn't trust in them because he didn't go to them for advice, did he? Verses 11-14 say:

> *So they put slave masters over them to oppress them with forced labor, and they built Pithom and Rameses as store cities for Pharaoh. But the more they were oppressed, the more they multiplied and*

spread; so the Egyptians came to dread the Israelites and worked them ruthlessly. They made their lives bitter with hard labor in brick and mortar and with all kinds of work in the fields; in all their hard labor the Egyptians used them ruthlessly.

Oh, and Pharaoh thought of more to do. He told the Hebrew midwives that when they delivered Israelite boys to kill them, but to let the baby girls live (as they could use them to produce more Egyptians). In verses 17-21, it says that the midwives, however, feared God and just couldn't do that, and that God blessed them because they feared Him. So Pharaoh came up with yet another plan. In verse 22, Pharaoh gave orders to all his people: *"Every boy that is born you must throw into the Nile, but let every girl live."* ✞

I have two sons, and that decree sends chills up my spine every time I read it. All I could think of is the pain and agony in every mother's heart, and I shudder. I'll tell you, if this doesn't show the hardness and coldness of a heart without God, I don't know what does. But as we go further in this study, we will find that we have just touched the surface on this subject of sin separating us from God.

Talk about a sense of hopelessness for these Israelites! Here they were suffering as slaves, enduring hard labor day after day, and now they had to deal with the killing of all their baby boys. How could they stand it any longer? I love this truthful fact that when all looks hopeless, God is right around the corner. In Chapter 2, one can see the hand of God—His gracious plan in motion. All is NEVER hopeless with an Almighty God. I remember the words God said to Abraham and Sarah in Genesis 18:14a, where He made them ask themselves, *"Is anything too hard for the LORD?"*

Do you notice that God makes us answer that same question ourselves? It's like, well, do you really believe He is God or not? Jesus says in Luke 18:27, *"What is impossible with men is possible with God."*

Remembering is a good thing. It keeps us on our toes and reminds us of experiences that show where we failed on our own and then all looked impossible. But when we allow God to step in, nothing IS impossible. I remember many years ago, one of my brothers, who I love and respect more than words can say, fell into an alcohol dependency problem. Do you understand that it takes only one drink to start a life as an alcoholic? It takes only one drink to start an addiction that can ruin one's own life, as well as the lives of others. I have NO doubt that the Lord had His protective, loving hand on my brother, just like He did with the Israelites. It just didn't look like it at the time. We sometimes forget that God's timing is perfect, and He is doing mighty things during our "waiting." For an alcoholic to seek help, it usually takes an experience that will cause him or her to hit rock bottom. I know you have heard this before, but one has to want help before he or she will accept it. So a rock bottom experience can help in the process. My brother had one of those experiences, and then he went into rehab for treatment. It was brutal, not just for him, but for our family. There were so many emotions involved. Stories came out that were hurtful. I hated that because I thought we were there to be loving and supportive. Apparently, according to mentors, this is all part of the process. Oh, but there where some great moments, too. I certainly do not want to discourage anyone from seeking help. But at my brother's "graduation," he was given a coin, which he would always carry in his pocket as a reminder of his addiction and to help him be strong when tempted. The coin was passed from person to person around the room. When we received the coin, we each had to say something positive, loving, and encouraging. I know that any addiction is BIGGER than ourselves. They were taught that also, and the first of the "twelve steps" for recovery states there is a higher power greater than you. When it was my turn to speak, I said without ANY hesitation and with all my heart that there is only ONE higher power, and He is the ONLY One bigger than the power of addiction inside of you. So the best thing for help and encouragement for my brother that I could say were these words from God's Word. I remember looking at him with more love than I had ever had for him, and knowing that I had THE one and ONLY answer for him. Not that I am so smart, but God certainly is! I quoted Psalm 121, and it says:

> *1I lift up my eyes to the hills—*
> *where does my help come from?*
> *2My help comes from the LORD,*

the Maker of heaven and earth.
3He will not let your foot slip—
    he who watches over you will not slumber;
4indeed, he who watches over Israel
    will neither slumber nor sleep.

5The LORD watches over you—
    the LORD is your shade at your right hand;
6the sun will not harm you by day,
    nor the moon by night.

7The LORD will keep you from all harm—
    he will watch over your life;
8the LORD will watch over your coming and going
    both now and forevermore.

When all looks hopeless, God is not sleeping. He is up to something. Read this tender story of God's protective hand at work and the beginning of His deliverance plan to free His people from their Egyptian bondage. Yes, it was still going to take 80 years, but it was the start.

1Now a man of the house of Levi married a Levite woman, 2and she became pregnant and gave birth to a son. When she saw that he was a fine child, she hid him for three months. 3But when she could hide him no longer, she got a papyrus basket for him and coated it with tar and pitch. Then she placed the child in it and put it among the reeds along the bank of the Nile. 4His sister stood at a distance to see what would happen to him.

5Then Pharaoh's daughter went down to the Nile to bathe, and her attendants were walking along the river bank. She saw the basket among the reeds and sent her slave girl to get it. 6She opened it and saw the baby. He was crying, and she felt

*sorry for him. "This is one of the Hebrew babies,"
she said.*

*7Then his sister asked Pharaoh's daughter,
"Shall I go and get one of the Hebrew women to
nurse the baby for you?"*

*8"Yes, go," she answered. And the girl went
and got the baby's mother. 9Pharaoh's daughter
said to her, "Take this baby and nurse him for me,
and I will pay you." So the woman took the baby
and nursed him. 10When the child grew older, she
took him to Pharaoh's daughter and he became her
son. She named him Moses, saying, "I drew him out
of the water"* (Exodus 2:1-10).

What, you say? It took EIGHTY years to get the man of
God's choosing prepared for the job? Yes, it did! Think about it. Do
you think that you and I are just born ready to serve? I'm laughing
out loud right now as I write this as I think of my own life. Guess
what? It takes some pretty hard knocks over the head in life to
physically and spiritually grow up into what God has created us for.
Because He does have something in mind! He has created every one
of us, believe it or not, not for ourselves but for Him. Every day is a
preparation for how He can and will use us tomorrow. Remember,
God does not call the equipped, He equips the called.

After Moses lived and learned in the house of Pharaoh for 40
years, let's follow the next course of action in God's molding and
preparation process in verses 11-22:

*11One day, after Moses had grown up, he
went out to where his own people were and watched
them at their hard labor. He saw an Egyptian
beating a Hebrew, one of his own people.
12Glancing this way and that and seeing no one, he
killed the Egyptian and hid him in the sand. 13The
next day he went out and saw two Hebrews fighting.
He asked the one in the wrong, "Why are you hitting
your fellow Hebrew?"*

14The man said, "Who made you ruler and judge over us? Are you thinking of killing me as you killed the Egyptian?" Then Moses was afraid and thought, "What I did must have become known."

15When Pharaoh heard of this, he tried to kill Moses, but Moses fled from Pharaoh and went to live in Midian, where he sat down by a well. 16Now a priest of Midian had seven daughters, and they came to draw water and fill the troughs to water their father's flock. 17Some shepherds came along and drove them away, but Moses got up and came to their rescue and watered their flock.

18When the girls returned to Reuel their father, he asked them, "Why have you returned so early today?"

19They answered, "An Egyptian rescued us from the shepherds. He even drew water for us and watered the flock."

20"And where is he?" he asked his daughters. "Why did you leave him? Invite him to have something to eat."

21Moses agreed to stay with the man, who gave his daughter Zipporah to Moses in marriage. 22Zipporah gave birth to a son, and Moses named him Gershom, saying, "I have become an alien in a foreign land."

Even though Moses had been raised as an Egyptian (which equipped him to understand them), he never forgot who he really was and where he came from. He always knew that he was as Israelite and that he would defend them even to death. However, when he had to flee for his life, why did he go to the desert of Midian of all places? Yes, it was remote. He probably thought that no one from Egypt would find him there. All of those are good answers, but God was leading him there all the time. God knew Moses' future and knew that he needed another 40 years to learn how to take care of sheep (which are not too smart) in the desert. It also gave him some much needed time to think. Do you get so busy sometimes, even with doing very good things, that you don't take the time to think about God? Do you think that an hour on Sunday morning is enough? I know HE doesn't think so.

> *Blessed is the man*
> > *who does not walk in the counsel of the wicked*
> *or stand in the way of sinners*
> *or sit in the seat of mockers.*
> *But his delight is in the law of the LORD,*
> > *and on his law he meditates day and night.*
> *He is like a tree planted by streams of water,*
> > *which yields its fruit in season*
> *and whose leaf does not wither.*
> > *Whatever he does prospers* (Psalm 1:1-3).

From my own experience, there have been many times where I could tell the Lord was saying to my spirit, "TIME OUT, remember ME?" I'm rather embarrassed, because I have been in ministry for many, many years. Sometimes I get so busy teaching Bible Study that I need a time out to rediscover who He really is and that He loves me enough to do whatever it takes for me to finally take that time out with Him. So next time He lands you "on your back" so to speak, check to see if it is because YOU just might need a time out with Him yourself.

After 80 years, it was time for God to tell Moses what he had been created, protected, and prepared to do. During this preparation time for Moses, and also for you and me, comes deprogramming of ourselves, our selfishness, and our self-centeredness. And then we are reprogrammed into someone who will LISTEN to His Voice and obey. Believe me when I say this: you will NEVER fulfill God's plan for your life unless you are willing to be reprogrammed by Him. All was ready; God's timing was crystal clear.

> *During that long period, the king of Egypt died. The Israelites groaned in their slavery and cried out, and their cry for help because of their slavery went up to God. God heard their groaning and he*

*remembered his covenant with Abraham, with Isaac
and with Jacob. So God looked on the Israelites and
was concerned about them* (Exodus 2:23-25).

Now, in Exodus 3:1-3, yes, it is time. Why? How else can
you explain a talking burning bush?

*Now Moses was tending the flock of Jethro his
father-in-law, the priest of Midian, and he led the
flock to the far side of the desert and came to
Horeb, the mountain of God. There the angel of the
LORD appeared to him in flames of fire from within
a bush. Moses saw that though the bush was on fire
it did not burn up. So Moses thought, "I will go
over and see this strange sight—why the bush does
not burn up."*

STOP! Did you see that? Another ordinary day started for
Moses. God is able to do some of His best calling on our ordinary
days. The only thing that wasn't ordinary was that a bush was on fire
but did not seem to be burning up. That needed to be checked out,
for sure. Curiosity got the best of Moses. God will do what He has
to do to get us over to where He can talk to us and get us to finally
listen. Listening for the Voice of God takes hearing it again and
again over time. Don't give up trying. Stay in His Word, get to
know Him better, and like any "sheep" you will get to know your
Shepherd's Voice and then will want to follow none other. *When the
LORD saw that he had gone over to look, God called to him from
within the bush, "Moses! Moses!" And Moses said, "Here I am"*
(v.4).

Notice what God called Moses. He called him by name.
Yes, He knows your name! He knows YOU. You are important to
Him, so He knows your name. Read verses 5-6:

*"Do not come any closer," God said. "Take off your
sandals, for the place where you are standing is
holy ground." Then he said, "I am the God of your
father, the God of Abraham, the God of Isaac and*

*the God of Jacob." At this, Moses hid his face,
because he was afraid to look at God.*

God wanted Moses to know just Who he was talking to so
that he would listen. I think we should have a "take off our sandals"
experience every now and then to remind us who God really is, like
Isaiah did in chapter 6:1-3:

> *In the year that King Uzziah died, I saw the Lord
> seated on a throne, high and exalted, and the train
> of his robe filled the temple. Above him were
> seraphs, each with six wings: With two wings they
> covered their faces, with two they covered their feet,
> and with two they were flying. And they were
> calling to one another:*
> *"Holy, holy, holy is the LORD Almighty; the whole
> earth is full of his glory."*

I'll tell you what, when I see the Lord like that, I have a
tendency to listen and realize Who He is. It's called humility, and
humility is simply knowing your place: He's God; you're not!
Moses heard God alright. He had ears, but he didn't like
what God had to say. Read verses 7-10:

> *The LORD said, "I have indeed seen the misery of
> my people in Egypt. I have heard them crying out
> because of their slave drivers, and I am concerned
> about their suffering. So I have come down to
> rescue them from the hand of the Egyptians and to
> bring them up out of that land into a good and
> spacious land, a land flowing with milk and honey--
> the home of the Canaanites, Hittites, Amorites,
> Perizzites, Hivites and Jebusites. And now the cry of
> the Israelites has reached me, and I have seen the
> way the Egyptians are oppressing them. So now, go.
> I am sending you to Pharaoh to bring my people the
> Israelites out of Egypt."*

I have to insert here that verses 7-8 really comfort me. Sometimes when I think that God feels distant, or that He is not answering, or that someone is getting away with something, or that He's taking too long, I read those verses. God said that He saw, He heard, He was concerned, and now He was coming down to rescue His people. It had been over 400 years! That was a long wait. But He was there all the time, keeping watch. Then, at just the right time, to the rescue He came. What a relief that is! Whatever is going on in your life right now, take comfort. You have a God who sees, hears, is concerned, and is going to come to the rescue at just the right time—not a minute before, not a minute after. But do you know what He is up to in the meantime? He's testing to see if you'll wait, trust, and obey. I can remember a time when Tom and I sensed that God was going to do something unique in our ministry, and yet all I was singing at was one little venue after another. While it didn't seem too exciting, we just kept plugging away, knowing that every concert had the opportunity for one soul to either be saved or encouraged.

One night we were in a church in Pompano Beach, Florida. It was a weeknight, and the only people there were those who came on a small bus from the area nursing care facility. It wasn't what we had in mind for this church service for that night. When you are willing to listen for God's Voice, He will give you what it takes to do what He's called you to do, even if it wasn't what you expected. I looked at those dear people and gave them one of the best concerts I ever gave. I held nothing back. I really don't know what it did for them, but I felt wonderful. I knew I did what God brought me there for, and how it was received into those old hearts was up to Him. The minister of that church, by listening to His Voice, later called his son-in-law, who was in the United States Air Force, involved with the Thunderbirds. That led to an invitation to sing for a whole weekend at Langley Air Force Base, which then led to many more opportunities on different bases across the country.

One thrill of my lifetime was singing "I'll Fly Away" on the flight line in front of 30,000 people. When I sang my last song, "Glory, Glory Hallelujah," the Thunderbirds took off right behind me. My heart almost came out of my chest. I also had the opportunity to talk and listen to a colonel (in an AWACS spy plane at Tinker Air Force Base) as he wept about his wife just leaving him and his son. I shared right there with him about Jesus and His love. I also got to watch God bring a Rabbi and his little boys to hear me sing songs about Jesus at another base. Later, they were found in the Protestant library.

I could go on and on. But my point is: we all need to believe that the Lord knows what He is doing when He is preparing us, making us wait, and doing what He has to do so that we will listen and fulfill the mission He has for us.

Unfortunately, verse 11 starts with the word "BUT." Do you know that you can say you believe God is able, that His timing is perfect, and that He has a plan for your life; and then if you say "BUT," you have placed a null and void stamp on everything you said previously? Listen to yourself telling either yourself or someone else how much faith you have in God and see how often you add a "BUT." Actually, you are really saying that you DON'T quite believe, and that is not enough in God's point of view. *The man who says, "I know him," but does not do what he commands is a liar, and the truth is not in him* (1 John 2:4).

So He will work with you on that. Do you remember a time when God called you for an assignment, and you said (or thought), "You want me to go where and do what!"? Now read some of Moses' excuses and how God was patient, encouraged him, and gave him the answers to his doubts in 3:11-15:

> *11But Moses said to God, "Who am I, that I should go to Pharaoh and bring the Israelites out of Egypt?"*
>
> *12And God said, "I will be with you. And this will be the sign to you that it is I who have sent you: When you have brought the people out of Egypt, you will worship God on this mountain."*
>
> *13Moses said to God, "Suppose I go to the Israelites and say to them, `The God of your fathers has sent me to you,' and they ask me, `What is his name?' Then what shall I tell them?"*

14God said to Moses, "I AM WHO I AM. This is what you are to say to the Israelites: `I AM has sent me to you.' " ✝

15God also said to Moses, "Say to the Israelites, `The LORD, the God of your fathers—the God of Abraham, the God of Isaac and the God of Jacob—has sent me to you.' This is my name forever, the name by which I am to be remembered from generation to generation."

I have given a lot of thought to God's saying that He is the "I Am." For as long as I can remember, I simply accepted it to mean that He alone is God and there is none other. But I believe His name is more personal than that. Those two words which describe Him have endless possibilities! You can fit a finishing sentence or another word to the "I Am," depending on your particular need for that day, minute, or second. I tried it. It works! If I feel insecure, He reassures me that, "I am your refuge and your fortress." When I need wisdom in a decision, He says to me, "I am your Counselor." And still more, "I am the One who will never leave you or forsake you." "I am the One who will give you comfort." "I am the One who loves you like no one else." See, there is no end to the "I AM." He is sufficient. He is enough. He is all you need. He is the "I AM."

This debate went on in chapter 4 also. In verse 13, Moses had the nerve to say to the Lord (and notice that the verse starts with a "but"), *But Moses said, "O Lord, please send someone else to do it."* The following verse said that the Lord's anger burned. Yes, the Lord gets MAD! Does He stop loving us? Absolutely NOT! But He does get angry when we do not obey or trust Him. *We know that we have come to know him if we obey his commands* (1 John 2:3).

You will see this over and over as we study together in this book. The Lord gets the last word, always. He will accomplish His purpose. Moses, albeit with fear and trembling, finally complied. And that's what the Lord asks of any one of us. He's prepared us, reprogrammed us, and promises to lead us every step of the way—now MOVE IT!!

CHAPTER 2

JESUS' SIGNPOSTS

"Every Boy": ✟ Pg. 55

● …Matthew 2:16-18, *When Herod realized that he had been outwitted by the Magi, he was furious, and he gave orders to kill all the boys in Bethlehem and its vicinity who were two years old and under, in accordance with the time he had learned from the Magi. Then what was said through the prophet Jeremiah was fulfilled:*

> *"A voice is heard in Ramah,*
> *weeping and great mourning,*
> *Rachel weeping for her children*
> *and refusing to be comforted,*
> *because they are no more."*

Can't you see it? Whether in the Old Testament or New Testament, the quest for personal power, to be in control, is an ongoing battle driven by our sinful human nature. When will we realize we are to let go and let God?

"I Am": ✝ Pg. 65

● ...Mark 14:61b-62, *Again the high priest asked him, "Are you the Christ, the Son of the Blessed One?" "I am," said Jesus. "And you will see the Son of Man sitting at the right hand of the Mighty One and coming on the clouds of heaven."*

● ...John 18:4-6, *Jesus, knowing all that was going to happen to him, went out and asked them, "Who is it you want?" "Jesus of Nazareth," they replied. "I am he," Jesus said. (And Judas the traitor was standing there with them.) When Jesus said, "I am he," they drew back and fell to the ground.*

● ...Revelation 1:8, *"I am the Alpha and the Omega," says the Lord God, "who is, and who was, and who is to come, the Almighty."*

● ...Revelation 1:17b-18, *Then he placed his right hand on me and said: "Do not be afraid. I am the First and the Last. I am the Living One; I was dead, and behold I am alive for ever and ever! And I hold the keys of death and Hades.*

Lesson 2: God Prepares His Man for the Job
Exodus 1 - 4:17

1.   How did God bless His nation of Israel?

2.   What was Pharaoh afraid of? How did he intend to handle the problem? (1:10.)

3.   How dangerous is it when "self" is the most important person in your life? What are the results?

4.   How dangerous is a continuous negative attitude? What does it say about the heart?

5.   What were Pharaoh's negative schemes?

6.   Who was Moses? How do you see that God already had a plan in motion for Moses from 2:1-10?

7.   Do you ever say the word "lucky" or "coincidence"? Do you believe in those words OR in God's plan because it cannot be both? How should that affect the way you live?

8.   Why did Moses flea to Midian? What happened there?

9.   What do you believe about God's timetable?

10. Explain Moses' burning bush experience. What did God want to remind Moses about Himself?

11. What is very comforting about 3:7-8?

12.   What does God ask Moses to do and what does He promise
       Moses? Yet, how did Moses respond? What was, then,
       God's response? (4:14.)

13.   What is God's name? Why is that His name?

14.   Why is He your "I AM" today?

3

Leaving for Egypt

Moses and his family left their home in Midian and started their journey to Egypt. In Exodus 4:20 it reads, *So Moses took his wife and sons, put them on a donkey and started back to Egypt. And he took the staff of God in his hand.* (God told him to do that in chapter 4:17.)

In 4:21-23, the Lord told Moses exactly what was going to transpire.

> *The LORD said to Moses, "When you return to Egypt, see that you perform before Pharaoh all the wonders I have given you the power to do. But I will harden his heart so that he will not let the people go. Then say to Pharaoh, `This is what the LORD says: Israel is my firstborn son, and I told you, "Let my son go, so he may worship me." But you refused to let him go; so I will kill your firstborn son.'"*

There is something in that verse I have not been able to understand until this study. Why would God harden Pharaoh's heart when the whole idea was to get the people out? That verse distinctly says that God would harden Pharaoh's heart. When we get to the ten plagues, it will become clearer. You see, there had to be ALL of the ten plagues. Every plague represented a judgment on Egypt's gods. God was going to prove to them that HE alone is God and that their so-called gods were a joke. There were times when Pharaoh softened during the time of the plagues, and you will read how the Lord hardened his heart so he wouldn't let the people go. I always thought that after a plague was lifted, Pharaoh simply changed his mind because of his stubbornness. NO, that was God's doing! Not only were the plagues to show Egypt, but also Israel for that matter, Who He was and is, by getting to that tenth plague. It was the blood of the sacrificed lamb on the doorpost which was going to deliver Israel from Egypt, not frogs or gnats. Then it dawned on me (thank you, Holy Spirit) that there is NO deliverance from the bondage of sin other than the blood of Christ shed on the cross. I believe there were a few of those plagues where Pharaoh would have let them leave before they happened, but God hardened his heart because the completeness of the plagues and His purposes for them had to be accomplished, not only for the Israelites, but for us today.

Let's return to Moses' journey back to Egypt. After a day's journey, they stopped for the night. Read this in 4:24, *At a lodging place on the way, the LORD met Moses and was about to kill him.*

I can't tell you how many times I read that verse. It just didn't make any sense. God had just spent 80 years preparing this man for this mission and NOW is about to kill him. That's a lot of investment time for naught! Why in the world would He do that NOW? Then it became clear that Moses had failed to circumcise his sons. That was very serious, because God had commanded circumcision to be the visible sign of His chosen people—that every male be circumcised as a symbol of the covenant He made with Abraham. Moses' failure to do that was sheer disobedience. Basically, God was saying that if Moses would not obey that command, he would no doubt not obey others either. And God needed someone who would listen to Him and obey what He told him to do. There was no way Moses could be the leader of this HUGE mission if he chose to do it his way, not God's way. God was very clear here. He would rather kill Moses and start all over than use someone who was only half committed. Wow, that's a lesson, isn't it? And do you know what? God hasn't changed His mind on that. No, He might not literally kill us, but He will kill the opportunity for us to experience an exciting moment in time where we see His hand willing to work through us.

The Bible doesn't say why Moses hadn't circumcised his sons; but as I studied the life of Moses, I couldn't help but see that there was difficulty in that marriage of Moses and Zipporah. Back in chapter 2, it seemed that Moses got married to Jethro's daughter mighty fast. Now remember, Moses admitted that he had become an alien in a foreign land (2:22). He married outside his faith. Marriage is hard enough, but with different faiths it is next to impossible. That is why the apostle Paul gave some great and powerful advice on the subject:

> *Do not be yoked together with unbelievers. For what*
> *do righteousness and wickedness have in common?*
> *Or what fellowship can light have with darkness?*
> *What harmony is there between Christ and Belial?*
> *What does a believer have in common with an*
> *unbeliever?* [Belial is a word Paul used for Satan.]
> (II Corinthians 6:14-15.)

I'm going to venture out and say that Moses and Zipporah were unevenly yoked. Moses knew the details of God's covenant with Abraham concerning circumcision (Genesis 17:9-14), but my guess is when he tried to talk to her about it, she considered it as mutilation, bloody, and gory, and NO way was that going to happen to her boys. I think Moses, as we say today, had to pick his battles with her, and he thought maybe he could slip that one by. I mean, who was really going to notice? Was Moses more afraid of his wife than of his God? It raises a good point about when we are up against God's commands and we have the tendency to compromise. It is so tempting, because who wants trouble in the family, right? You never saw Zipporah as the helpmate to Moses that he could have used. Remember when God told Adam in Genesis 2:18, *The LORD God said, "It is not good for the man to be alone. I will make a helper suitable for him."*

There was a point in the Exodus when Moses sent Zipporah back to her father. Call me crazy, but I just think that was not a good union, and she was not willing to be the wife to Moses that he needed.

Can't you see why it is so important to SEEK the Lord before picking a partner for marriage? Jesus said in Matthew 7:7 that if we seek we will find. When it comes to your belief in Jesus, both you and your partner have to be moving in the same direction. Have you ever wondered if you married the wrong person, or discovered he or she was not what you had expected, or he or she changed and is not the same person you married? I think we might become disillusioned by thinking that God hand picks our mate for us. Now, before you misunderstand, He knows who our mate will be, but He gives us our choice to pick one. He'll work with us on our choice. But, the principle is the same. He'll let us choose whomever we want, but the command is that He is the head and controller of that union, and the two are to walk hand in hand with Him. Sounds almost euphoric, doesn't it?

> *Though one may be overpowered,*
> *two can defend themselves.*
> *A cord of three strands is not quickly broken.*
> (Ecclesiastes 4:12.)

Let me tell you a story about a couple I met in my travels. I noticed this young woman at church, and she was everywhere doing everything. Wherever there was a need, she was Johnny-on-the-spot to get the job done. Her sweet service was very noticeable, even to me, a stranger. Oh, when I see people like that, I have to talk to them, because a servant's heart does not come without a story. I wanted to know hers. When I approached her, she was very shy— she could hardly look at me when we talked. I didn't get much out of her at that time except a little smile and a thank you when I told her what I saw. I didn't push the matter. Later, I saw a man with the same kind of spirit going around the church getting everything ready. He was more talkative, and I found out that he was married to the gal with whom I had just talked. I say this in all kindness, just to give you a visual, but they were simple, no frills, and rather plain people outwardly. But, when you got up close to both of them, they radiated His Light that can only come from within.

When we went downstairs for dinner after the service, I was able to get to know them better. I found out that he had made some very bad choices and had landed in prison for quite a long time. He was a mess, and life did not look so good from his position. She told me that everyone told her to divorce him so she and their children could get on with their lives. She went on to say that she just couldn't because the Lord did not tell her to do so. So, choosing to listen to the Lord rather than everyone else, she stayed and waited for years until he was released. That unconditional love and grace was such a testimony to him that, while still in prison, he gave his life to the Lord and allowed the Lord to make a new creature out of him. And did He EVER! Both had tears in their eyes. Their one son (a teenager, by the way) stood with his arm around his dad with such respect and admiration that it brought me to tears. Then she said something to me that I will never forget. She said, "If I would have left him, look what I would have missed!" Do you think that she wondered a few times if she had married the wrong person? I'm sure of it. But she made her choice and now was willing to let the Lord work with her on it. She was an obedient, humble servant willing to wait for the Lord to change her husband's heart, and now together they walk hand in hand with the Lord.

They are, in my opinion, the perfect couple because they are yoked with the Lord and with each other. That's what God created marriage to be. Will there be difficulties? Without question! But at the top of the triangle, which has only One point by the way, together both sides meet there. There's a solution there every time.

When Moses and Aaron (his brother whom God sent to help him) went to Pharaoh as we read in chapter 5 and told them of God's intent to deliver Israel from the Egyptians, Pharaoh let his power go to his head; instead of letting them leave, he made it worse for them. (All those Pharaohs had such control issues!) We know that this is all in God's control, Who, don't ever forget, is the Master Controller of all things! Again, Moses shows his spiritual immaturity by having a "spiritual tantrum." After hearing from the foremen on how bad it had gotten, Moses went to the Lord and shook his "little spiritual fists" at Him and said:

> *"O Lord, why have you brought trouble upon this people? Is this why you sent me? Ever since I went to Pharaoh to speak in your name, he has brought trouble upon this people, and you have not rescued your people at all"* (Exodus 5:22b-23).

Can't you just see Moses and hear him blame God for not doing what He said? Oh, oh, oh, when are we going to let God be

God and trust what He says? God warned him that it was going to be like this. There really should not have been any surprises here. Listen to how the Lord came back with His response in chapter 6:1-8:

> *1Then the* LORD *said to Moses, "Now you will see what I will do to Pharaoh: Because of my mighty hand he will let them go; because of my mighty hand he will drive them out of his country."*
>
> *2God also said to Moses, "I am the* LORD. *3I appeared to Abraham, to Isaac and to Jacob as God Almighty, but by my name the* LORD *I did not make myself known to them. 4I also established my covenant with them to give them the land of Canaan, where they lived as aliens. 5Moreover, I have heard the groaning of the Israelites, whom the Egyptians are enslaving, and I have remembered my covenant.*
>
> *6"Therefore, say to the Israelites: 'I am the* LORD, *and I will bring you out from under the yoke of the Egyptians. ✝ I will free you from being slaves to them, and I will redeem you with an outstretched arm and with mighty acts of judgment. 7I will take you as my own people, and I will be your God. Then you will know that I am the* LORD *your God, who brought you out from under the yoke of the Egyptians. 8And I will bring you to the land I swore with uplifted hand to give to Abraham, to Isaac and to Jacob. I will give it to you as a possession. I am the* LORD.'"

Studying God's Word and reading it are two different things. I want you to study these verses. When you are willing to do that, you will see how many times God says, "I am" and "I will." I wish I could hear every one of you tell me what that means to you. Anytime you are discouraged, wavering, doubting, or just plain full of despair, THESE are the verses, if you choose to study them, that will lift you up. They are powerful. They are true. This is YOUR God who is talking to you. *But Moses said to the LORD, "If the Israelites will not listen to me, why would Pharaoh listen to me, since I speak with faltering lips?"* (6:12.)

Moses showed us that we have a choice to either only hear God's Word or to live it and believe it. The verse starts with a "but" and an "if." It doesn't sound like he chose to believe God's Word, does it? That, my friend, is a sign of lack of faith, which is really not knowing Him well enough, and is immature faith, which God, in His patience, purpose, and plan will correct—in Moses and in you and me. Believe me, the Lord told Moses just what He was going to do. Moses was going to be a part of it, and it would change Moses.

Moses and Aaron went to Pharaoh again and warned him. Moses shares with Pharaoh what the Lord had said to him directly in 7:5, *"And the Egyptians will know that I am the LORD when I stretch out my hand against Egypt and bring the Israelites out of it."*

God warned Pharaoh good! Here are the ten plagues, and I will try to explain how each plague was designed to expose the ineptitude of Egypt's so-called gods.

1. Nile turned into blood. The Nile was sacred to the Egyptians. Egyptians gods were associated with the river. Osiris was one of the chief gods and was primarily the god of the Nile. The Egyptians believed that the river was his bloodstream.

2. Frogs. They represented Heka, a frog-headed goddess of fertility and rebirth.

3. Gnats. Represents the earth god, Geb. This god was closely related to the earth in all of its states.

4. Flies. They were most likely the sacred beetle or scarab. These scarabs, many of gold, are found in the tombs of Egypt. They were sacred to the sun-god Ra. Many insects were identified with goddesses and gods and were worshiped.

5.   Killing of the livestock. Egypt mummified their bulls. Apis, the black bull, was worshiped in Egypt. It is interesting that when the Israelites thought that Moses was lost on Mt. Sinai, they gave their gold to be made into a calf in the image of Apis (Exodus 32:3-4). Closely related to the worship of Apis was that of Hathor, the cow goddess of fertility. Even with all her powers, why couldn't Hathor keep the sacred cows alive during this plague?

6.   Boils. The priests who served in the Egyptian temples had to be clean, without any type of breakout or sickness. This brought to a halt all of the false worship in Egypt. Where were the healing gods of Egypt?

7.   Hail. This plague was directed against Isis (sometimes represented as cow-headed), goddess of fertility and considered the goddess of the air. The tears of Isis falling into the Nile River caused it to overflow its banks bringing nourishment to the land.

8.   Locusts. Locusts are used in Scripture as a picture of judgment (see Revelation 9:1-10). It is probably one of the worst things man has to face. Where were the gods of fields and harvests?

        There was a systematic way God was dealing with the Egyptians. First, the plagues were directed against the different gods, goddesses, and idols that infested the land. Now, in the final two plagues, God was going to use them to bring tremendous hardship upon the people.

9.   Darkness. This judgment was upon the sun god, Ra, Thoth, the moon god, Horus, often pictured by a winged sun disk, and Harakhte, another form of Horus. Darkness came over the land of Egypt in the daytime. The sun disc was the most familiar symbol Egyptians used; it is in all of their art. This plague showed the utter helplessness of Ra.

10.   Death of the firstborn. The firstborn of both man and beast belonged to the gods of Egypt. The Lord God will claim the first fruits of the Egyptian gods (12:22-23). Where was the power of Pharaoh, the "perfect god"? It was nonexistent, since the son of Pharaoh, the next god, was among those who had been killed. The animal gods were just as helpless, for even the cows and bulls were being killed.

What God says, He does! Read 12:29-30:

> *At midnight the LORD struck down all the firstborn in Egypt, from the firstborn of Pharaoh, who sat on the throne, to the firstborn of the prisoner, who was in the dungeon, and the firstborn of all the livestock as well. Pharaoh and all his officials and all the Egyptians got up during the night, and there was loud wailing in Egypt, for there was not a house without someone dead.*

As sad an event as this was, I am always in awe of God's power. Certainly even the family members knew who all the firstborn were. But God knew even the firstborn of all the livestock in the fields or barns!

I have no words to say after that. It speaks for itself. But I would ask you to look at the impact of this event from a personal perspective. First, let's clarify from Exodus 11:4-5 who was to die that night:

> *So Moses said, "This is what the LORD says: `About midnight I will go throughout Egypt. very firstborn son in Egypt will die, from the firstborn son of Pharaoh, who sits on the throne, to the firstborn son of the slave girl, who is at her hand mill, and all the firstborn of the cattle as well.'"*

Now I would ask you. Think of all the firstborn sons now living in your immediate family, extended family, and your friendship circles. Remember, this could be your great grandfather, grandfather, father, husband, son, grandson, uncle, cousin, dearest friend, or yourself. When you go to sleep tonight and awake tomorrow—think of the devastation of finding out who you had lost during the night!

God had given the Israelites strict instructions on how to prevent death in their homes. This will take some time, but just read how detailed the Passover was and still is today. Look at the detail in chapter 12:3-13:

> "*3 Tell the whole community of Israel that on the tenth day of this month each man is to take a lamb for his family, one for each household. 4 If any household is too small for a whole lamb, they must share one with their nearest neighbor, having taken into account the number of people there are. You are to determine the amount of lamb needed in accordance with what each person will eat. 5 The animals you choose must be year-old males without defect, and you may take them from the sheep or the goats. 6 Take care of them until the fourteenth day of the month, when all the people of the community of Israel must slaughter them at twilight. 7 Then they are to take some of the blood and put it on the sides and tops of the doorframes of the houses where they eat the lambs. 8 That same night they are to eat the meat roasted over the fire, along with bitter herbs, and bread made without yeast. 9 Do not eat the meat raw or cooked in water, but roast it over the fire— head, legs and inner parts. 10 Do not leave any of it till morning; if some is left till morning, you must burn it. 11 This is how you are to eat it: with your cloak tucked into your belt, your sandals on your feet and your staff in your hand. Eat it in haste; it is the LORD's Passover.*

12 "On that same night I will pass through Egypt and strike down every firstborn—both men and animals—and I will bring judgment on all the gods of Egypt. I am the LORD. 13 The blood will be a sign for you on the houses where you are; and when I see the blood, I will pass over you. No destructive plague will touch you when I strike Egypt." ♰

Then, later on in the chapter, God clearly told the Israelites how they were to commemorate this event yearly and how important it was that they pass this story down to their descendents:

"Obey these instructions as a lasting ordinance for you and your descendants. When you enter the land that the LORD will give you as he promised, observe this ceremony. And when your children ask you, 'What does this ceremony mean to you?' then tell them, 'It is the Passover sacrifice to the LORD, who passed over the houses of the Israelites in Egypt and spared our homes when he struck down the Egyptians'" (Exodus 12:24-27a).

This is certainly a lesson on how important it is for us to pass on the story of Jesus to our children. Of course, you can't give them something you don't have; but if you have Jesus in your heart, and you have experienced Him change your life through the power of the Holy Spirit, you CANNOT keep quiet. I will end this chapter by asking this question: "If we say we love our children, and in fact would give our lives for them, then why don't we show, tell, demonstrate, live out, and proclaim the precious, gracious story of our Savior?" What better gift can we give them?

CHAPTER 3

JESUS'  SIGNPOSTS

"The Yoke": ✞ Pg. 78

● ...Matthew 11:28-30, *"Come to me, all you who are weary and burdened, and I will give you rest. Take my yoke upon you and learn from me, for I am gentle and humble in heart, and you will find rest for your souls. For my yoke is easy and my burden is light."*

"The Blood": ✞ Pg. 83

● ...1 Corinthians 5:7b, *For Christ, our Passover lamb, has been sacrificed.*

● ...Romans 5:9, *Since we have now been justified by <u>his blood</u>, how much more shall we be saved from God's wrath through him!*

● ...Ephesians 1:7-8, *In him [Jesus] we have redemption through <u>his blood</u>, the forgiveness of sins, in accordance with the riches of God's grace that he lavished on us with all wisdom and understanding.*

●...1 Peter 1:18-19, *For you know that it was not with perishable things such as silver or gold that you were redeemed from the empty way of life handed down to you from your forefathers, but with the <u>precious blood</u> of Christ, a lamb without blemish or defect.*

*Underline, bold, bracket inserts, additional emphasis mine.

Lesson 3: Leaving for Egypt
Exodus 4:18 - Exodus 13:16

1. What do you think Moses was feeling as he began that calling?

2. After 80 years of preparation, why was God going to kill Moses? Why was circumcision so important to God?

3. What seemed to happen after Moses and Aaron spoke to Pharaoh?

4. What is a spiritual tantrum? What is the root problem when you have one of those? Do you think Moses had one in 5:22-23?

5. What does God promise Moses in chapter 6? What does God repeatedly say? What should that mean to Moses and you?

6. What will a "yea, but...." do to your testimony of faith and trust in an almighty God?

7. Name the ten plagues. What did God want to demonstrate to the Egyptians and the Israelites through those plagues?

8. What did the ten plagues represent?

9. Why did God harden Pharaoh's heart sometimes? What was the ultimate goal in those plagues? Why did God have to take Israel and Egypt through all ten?

10. What was the Passover? What does it represent?

11.   What was God's instruction to Israel in 13:14? Why was God so firm on that instruction?

12.   What are you showing by your life and teaching with your mouth to your loved ones who are watching and listening so closely? Is your life very convincing for the cause of Christ? If you were arrested for being a Christian, would there be enough evidence to convict you?

4

The Trip is On

The Israelites were on their way! This gets interesting right off the bat. In Exodus 13:17-18a we read:

> *When Pharaoh let the people go, God did not lead them on the road through the Philistine country, though that was shorter. For God said, "If they face war, they might change their minds and return to Egypt." So God led the people around by the desert road toward the Red Sea.*

A million-plus people were just embarking on a 225-mile trip by a direct route, but God took them the long way. Oh, but does He ever know us! He certainly knew them and what was ahead, and that they were going to be whining that song of actually missing Egypt many, many times in the future. So He knew the best path— this would require a long learning curve. If they had confronted their enemy, the Philistines, who would be a thorn in their flesh for this whole journey and for years after, by taking an alternate route, they would be running scared "right out of the gate." God knows us so well that He has a path that's better than ours, and it doesn't necessarily always seem to make sense at the time. Have you ever thought that God did not answer your request quickly enough? And when the answer came, was it a far different one than you had planned on? Oh come on, that's a big AMEN from all of us. Well, these couple of verses let me see God's protection, His better plan, and that He has my best interest in mind. You know what? God IS smarter than we are. He knows where we are weak and knows when we will be tempted to "cave" and fall backward, and that is NEVER

God's direction for us. It is ALWAYS forward. A couple of my favorite verses are in Philippians 3:13b -14 where the apostle Paul says:

> *But one thing I do: Forgetting what is behind and straining toward what is ahead, I press on toward the goal to win the prize for which God has called me heavenward in Christ Jesus.*

Friends, in Jesus' name we press on, and that sounds like a forward motion to me.

I can't forget to tell you how that whole mob knew where to go. God thinks of everything. Moses was just one man, and there were a ton of people not able to see him at one time. In chapter 13:21, it says:

> *By day the LORD went ahead of them in a pillar of cloud to guide them on their way and by night in a pillar of fire to give them light, so that they could travel by day or night.* ✞

Wouldn't that be great to see God's leading so clearly because He gave us a pillar of cloud by day, and a pillar of fire at night? HE DID! He is called the Holy Spirit. The very Spirit of God has been given to you and me on the day of our salvation to do just that. We can see clearly if we are just willing to let Him lead. Listen to what Jesus said to his disciples before He left this earth when they were scared to death to have Him leave them. He's been their guide to follow for three years, and now He's leaving them! *But when he, the Spirit of truth, comes, he will guide you into all truth* (John 16:13a). Doesn't that sound like the perfect guide to follow in order to reach Jesus' chosen destination for us?

Look where they landed: smack in front of the huge Red Sea. And they couldn't turn back, because Pharaoh changed his mind (all a part of God's plan and timing) and sent the best of his military after them. The Israelites could practically hear the hoofs a-comin'. Did they ever have words for poor Moses!

They said to Moses, "Was it because there were no graves in Egypt that you brought us to the desert to die? What have you done to us by bringing us out of Egypt? Didn't we say to you in Egypt, `Leave us alone; let us serve the Egyptians'? It would have been better for us to serve the Egyptians than to die in the desert!" (14:11-12.)

I'll tell you, that first part is sarcasm at its best—no graves in Egypt—they are known for their tombs and pyramids, for crying out loud. And then the later part about saying to Moses that they had told him to leave them in Egypt. Maybe I shouldn't say this, but I am: What in the world were they smoking? They were being tortured day after day! How quickly they forgot. But Moses' answer was nothing short of tremendous, courageous, and patient. It reveals acute faith. Now that's a changed Moses! In 14:13-14, we read:

Moses answered the people, "Do not be afraid. Stand firm and you will see the deliverance the LORD *will bring you today. The Egyptians you see today you will never see again. The* LORD *will fight for you; you need only to be still."*

It wasn't that long ago when God called him on this mission that he was full of excuses and even asked to be excused. You see, that's what surrender to an Almighty God will do to you. It will take your low self-worth, feelings of inadequacy, and doubt (the real killer), and turn you into someone who knows his or her God and knows He is capable of accomplishing the impossible, even when we certainly can't.

Can you believe it? He had no idea how God was going to do it; he just believed He would because God promised Abraham a promised land. I'm working on that kind of trust and faith; how about you? Well, you'd better really want it, because it doesn't come easy.

It had to take great faith, because when God told Moses to raise his staff and stretch out his hand over the sea so the water would divide and the Israelites would be able to go through the sea on dry ground, he did it! He simply did it! Of course, it happened just as God said it would, and the Israelites crossed on DRY ground, not mucky or an inch of water, but dry ground. When God says He is going to do something, He does it 100 percent. When they landed safely on the other side and the Egyptians started on their way through the sea, God dropped the wall of water, and not one of them survived. Did you ever wonder what the "changed" Moses was thinking as he watched all this? I have. There is no doubt in my mind what he was thinking; "Lord, thank you for knowing me best. Thank you for saying NO to my request to pick someone else for this job. I wouldn't have missed this for ANYTHING!"

When we are full of excuses when asked to serve the Lord in any way, do you ever stop and think of what you might miss? Excuses are just nice ways of saying we really don't want to do what is asked of us. We are too nice to come right out and say it, so we come up with some nice excuse to get us off the hook.

I had one of those "facing the Red Sea" kind of experiences a few years ago. We have a wonderful retirement community in downtown Holland, MI. My dad had a friend who lived there at the time. The facility had just gotten a brand new baby grand piano. Apparently my dad's friend told him that it was sad, because there it sat and no one played it. Naturally, my dad called me and TOLD me to get over there and play it. Even though I thought that was a might bold, this one never stops obeying her dad. One day, rather sheepishly, I walked in there and asked whether anyone would mind if I played their piano. The lady quickly said that I could. Good. So far no problem! I sat down and started playing the good old hymns of the faith, and it didn't take long before I had an audience. We had such a good time that they asked me to come back and do it again, so I did.

After a few visits, the activities director heard that I taught Bible Studies and asked if I would come and teach the residents there because I had a good rapport with them. My first thought was the heartiest NO you would have ever heard. Fast and furious, my thought process was searching for every excuse in the book. I didn't want to do this. No way! However, one of the most important works of the Holy Spirit is to help you recall what you have learned. He planted the story of Moses into my mind at just that moment. It was like I could hear the Lord quietly warning me to not miss this blessing. I said I would do it, and what started out to be an eight-week course turned into three years. What a time I had! They were so wonderful, and many became friends.

But there was one man in particular—Walter. He came in every Wednesday morning in his special walker and sat in the same place every time—right next to me on my right. Even at 90 years old, he had an eagerness to learn more and more. He knew the Bible was a treasure chest full of discoveries that was bottomless. During one of the lessons, I remember just breaking into the song, "Amazing Grace," because it truly made the point I was trying to make. I noticed that while I was singing, Walter was working very hard at trying to get something out of his pocket. He had had a stroke, so some of the simplest movements were difficult for him. I surely didn't want to embarrass him by turning and looking, so I just kept singing. He finally achieved his goal. He pulled out his hanky. He needed his hanky to wipe the tears that were flowing down his cheeks and for his nose that was running. After the lesson, he waited until everyone had left (and that always took awhile), and then began to explain to me what happened. It was almost as if he was embarrassed, like most men would be, but he continued anyway. He told me that "Amazing Grace" awes him. Every time he hears it he is reminded of what he was, and what he is now because of that grace.

Experiences in life have a way of taking you to your next spiritual level. You always think that it has to be some grand and big thing; but in this case, it was a simple, 90-year-old man with a faith that made him sparkle like the stars. I remember grabbing that old man and telling him that I wanted to be just like him. He looked at me with the look of "Are you kidding me?" He had something so real. He knew His God so well and loved Him so much, and it was obvious. We went on with our conversation, and he asked me if I knew his greatest moment in life. Of course I didn't, but I expected him to say something about WWII, or his late wife, children, or some adventure. I was stunned when he answered, "Today." That threw me at first, because I knew how much he missed his precious Edna, knew the pain of losing a child in an accident, and how he had been a strong, independent man, but now was dependent on others. How could today be his best day? His reason was simply, "Because I am that much closer to seeing Jesus, the author of the grace that saved me."

That is when I knew why the Lord made sure I said yes to this request. I, like Moses, thought to myself, "I would never have wanted to miss this." Can you imagine the joy I had singing, "What a day that will be when Jesus we will see, when we look upon His face, the One who saved me by His grace" ✝ at Walter's memorial service?

Walter made a dent in my life that I will never forget; and to think I was ready with my list of excuses. Shame on me!

What an event that Red Sea experience was! What a day of rejoicing! In fact, in chapter 15, Moses and the Israelites sang to the Lord. Aren't you thrilled that the Lord gave us the gift of music to express our hearts? Well, that's just what they did. They sang up a storm in worship to their great God. In fact, in verses 20-21, Moses' sister, Miriam, took the tambourine in her hand, and all the women followed her with tambourines and dancing. You can almost hear Miriam singing to the excited crowd, *"Sing to the LORD, for he is highly exalted. The horse and its rider he has hurled into the sea"* (v.21b).

Where did they get those tambourines, anyway? There was no music store around. When they left Egypt, I am pretty sure they were told to travel light. How do you know what to take when you are so limited? How do you pack? It had to be what was of utmost importance. Well, I believe that Miriam knew her God, and she must have thought that along this journey they would need those tambourines. They were of utmost importance. Have you played yours lately? When was the last time "Amazing Grace" made you want to search for that "tambourine" and just wail on it? Thanks, Walter! Because of you, I love the sound of a tambourine.

AMAZING GRACE

John Newton

Amazing Grace, how sweet the sound,
That saved a wretch like me.
I once was lost but now am found,
Was blind, but now I see.

T'was Grace that taught my heart to fear.
And Grace, my fears relieved.
How precious did that Grace appear
The hour I first believed.

Through many dangers, toils and snares
I have already come;
'Tis Grace that brought me safe thus far
and Grace will lead me home.

The Lord has promised good to me.
His word my hope secures.
He will my shield and portion be,
As long as life endures.

Yea, when this flesh and heart shall fail,
And mortal life shall cease,
I shall possess within the veil,
A life of joy and peace.

When we've been there ten thousand years
Bright shining as the sun.
We've no less days to sing God's praise
Than when we've first begun.

CHAPTER 4

JESUS'   SIGNPOSTS

"Way and Light": ✝ Pg. 92

●...John 14:6, *Jesus answered, "I am the way and the truth and the life.*

●...John 8:12, *When Jesus spoke again to the people, he said, "I am the light of the world. Whoever follows me will never walk in darkness, but will have the light of life."*

"Upon His Face": ✝ Pg. 96

●...Revelation 22:3b-4, *The throne of God and of the Lamb will be in the city, and his servants will serve him. They will see his face, and his name will be on their foreheads.*

Lesson 4: The Trip is On
Exodus 13:17 - Exodus 15:21

1. Why didn't God let the Israelites take the shorter and easier route when they began their journey?

2. What is a desert? What does it take to survive there? Why do you need "desert" time once in awhile?

3. How did God lead them? Could they miss it? How does He lead you today? Can you miss the leading? If you follow the Spirit, will you go in the right direction?

4. Why did the Israelites feel "sandwiched" and in an impossible situation? Why would God lead them into that?

5. In 14:10-12, how did the Israelites respond? Why was there a tone of sarcasm?

6. Did Egypt still have a powerful hold on them? Why? What was missing here? Is it ever missing in your life? What's your first clue that it is missing?

7. How can you tell that Moses has allowed God to change his excuses, fear, and doubt, into true belief, courage, and strength? Do you have the same choice today?

8. What did God tell Moses to do? Did he do it? Is that a key ingredient? What happened when he did what God told him to do?

9. Through this familiar story, what is God trying to cement in your mind and way of thinking?

10.   What was Israel's reaction when they witnessed this miracle of God? Was this God's intent? OK then, is that what He is trying to do to you?

11.   What does God LOVE to hear? (Chapter 15)

12.   What are some of the key phrases in this chapter? Have you said any of those phrases to Him lately? Why or why not?

5

Grumblers Need Commands

Have you ever had a spiritual mountain top experience? I mean the kind where you were flying high? Things are going good and you are walking with God! And then CRASH! In Exodus 15:22-24, it tells us that it was just three days after their euphoric high that the Israelites hit a snag. They needed water, and what they found was bitter. Immediately the grumbling began. Yet all they had to do was ask! In James 4:2d it says, *You do not have, because you do not ask God.*

How come grumbling and complaining always seems to be our reaction before we go to the Lord? You got me! All I can say is that it certainly shows why our human nature needs redemption. Moses cried out to the Lord (good thing he had some sense to do the right thing), and the Lord simply showed Moses a piece of wood and told him to throw it into the water. The water ✞ became sweet. Just like that!

Now the water problem was solved, but there was another beauty lurking right around the corner. Again, just a short time after seeing the Lord provide water for them we read this in chapter 16:3:

> *The Israelites said to them, "If only we had died by the LORD's hand in Egypt! There we sat around pots of meat and ate all the food we wanted, but you have brought us out into this desert to starve this entire assembly to death."*

They had to be in fantasyland! I don't think that they ate from the banquet table in Egypt when they were slaves being tortured. The patience of the Lord is unexplainable. I know that every time I look into the mirror. But here He explains to Moses that He will supply them with manna.✞ But the instructions regarding how and when to gather the manna were very specific. That's the way the Lord works. He promises to supply our needs; but we have to do our part and listen, and then do what He says, just the way He says it. He's funny that way. (I mean that in a very respectful way.) He is very serious about His instructions. You are not allowed to follow them half way. He always has and always will demand our all. After the instructions, of course, there were some who paid no attention to Moses, and they simply went out and tried to do it their way. WRONG! They suffered the consequences.

> *Then Moses said to them, "No one is to keep any of it until morning."*
> *However, some of them paid no attention to Moses; they kept part of it until morning, but it was full of maggots and began to smell. So Moses was angry with them* (Exodus 16:19-20).

That's the standard command of God. Obedience reaps blessings. Disobey and you'll reap the consequences. It's not rocket science.

No sooner had God provided food than He again tested them with a water problem. God will keep testing us until we learn. I remember our son, Chad, telling us that when he went into Marine basic training, there were some cocky guys there who said they couldn't and wouldn't be broken down. Chad said he learned that the fast-breakdown process was easier because they <u>will</u> break you down somehow, someway, and it isn't pretty. The Marines break you down to rebuild you into the best Marine possible, and isn't that the kind of Marines we want facing our enemies? And the Lord will continue to do what He has to do to fulfill His goal of breaking us down of ourselves in order to rebuild us into pliable material to work with so He can mold us into what He has created us to be.

Instead of recalling what God had done by supplying their needs completely in the past, in chapter 17 their grumbling started all over again! In fact, they got so mad at Moses that he was afraid they were going to stone him. That's terrible! Again, God came through and told Moses to strike the rock, and water gushed forth. Seeing that, those Israelites still had the audacity to ask Moses, *"Is the LORD among us or not?"* (Exodus 17:7b.) Before we get too exasperated with these people, remember that we, too, often accuse God of not being there. Have you ever heard the phrase, "If you feel distant from God, He's not the One who moved"? You figure out the rest.

The Israelites traveled to their next very important destination: Mount Sinai. It was there that the Lord would give Moses the Law and the detailed instructions for service in the tabernacle. When they arrived, the Lord had strong words for Moses to give to the Israelites. In chapter 19:4-6 God said:

> *"'You yourselves have seen what I did to Egypt, and how I carried you on eagles' wings and brought you to myself. Now if you obey me fully and keep my covenant, then out of all nations you will be my treasured possession. Although the whole earth is mine, you will be for me a kingdom of priests and a holy nation.' These are the words you are to speak to the Israelites."*

What a special message from God Himself! To think He considered them to be His treasured possession with an opportunity to be for Him a kingdom of priests. Only two stipulations: ***Obey me FULLY and keep my covenant!***

To be God's treasured possession—I can understand that and desire it more than life itself. But to be for Him a kingdom of priests threw me. I knew I had heard that similar phrase in the New Testament. Sure enough! It's in 1 Peter 2:9-10:

> *But you are a chosen people, a royal priesthood, a holy nation, a people belonging to God, that you may declare the praises of him who called you out of darkness into his wonderful light. Once you were not a people, but now you are the people of God; once you had not received mercy, but now you have received mercy.*

God was talking about His chosen people, the Israelites, in Exodus, and Peter was talking about us in the New Testament. Because of Jesus, we have been engrafted into the holy nation, His treasured possession; and we, too, are to be priests. You see, priests were set apart for God. They were mediators between God and the people. They would meet humans' needs on God's behalf. They did not touch unclean things. They mediated for God, showing and revealing His love and compassion to the people. Yes, I see it. Because of Jesus, we are to be priests through the power of the Holy Spirit living in us. We are to put God on display in our lives. We are the mediator between God and the world. We are to have the character of Christ and meet humans' needs on God's behalf. I haven't seen a chicken casserole come flying out of heaven onto a needy family's table, have you? We are to show God's love and compassion. The apostle Paul says that God promises to supply all our needs according to His riches in glory. (See Philippians 4:19.) How does God do that? He has extraordinary ways, and then sometimes He just uses His priests. Get it?

God was now going to give Moses the Ten Commandments. Why are they called commands? Probably because they are NOT suggestions! These commands are like a fence that God puts around us. If you stay inside the fence of God's protection and commands, you will be fine. If you think that you know better and you jump the fence, you subject yourself to great consequences when you encounter your enemy and this whole world around you. It's a dangerous, slippery slope outside that fence, and you will slip fast. People who say that Christianity is just a bunch of do's and don'ts absolutely do not understand God's love. He loves us so much, and He knows our weaknesses better than we do, so He is willing to fence us in with the Ten Commandments.

When I was a child, the minister would read the Scriptures from the King James Version. Now, I know there are many people who still believe that it is the ONLY version a Christian should study from. And that's fine if that's your version of choice. I remember once a lady called me and told me she had heard from someone that any other version of the Bible other than the King James was wrong, so she was going to have a great big bonfire and burn every other Bible version that she had in her house. I told her to hold on and think about it for a minute. Let's get realistic here. If you are reading a version of the Bible, (which King James is, also), it is NOT the version giving you the understanding of the Truth, but the Holy Spirit. I find that we all have our favorites, given our ability to read and comprehend, but it is only the Holy Spirit who can illuminate our hearts and minds. Saying that though, I have to admit that when our minister would read the Ten Commandments and would shout, "THOU SHALT NOT," as a little one, I believed he meant it! And the thing is, GOD DOES MEAN IT, no matter what version you read it in. The Ten Commandments are given out of love because God knows us so well. He knows what our sinful human nature is like, so He has to fence us in to keep us out of trouble—and we DO get into trouble! When? Well, when we jump the fence. Again, now listen to me; God's commands are NOT complicated. Stay in the fence and be safe, or think that you know better and jump the fence, and then as sure as shootin' you're going down. Trouble is around every corner.

But, you say, the commands are so old and outdated. Guess what? God hasn't changed. He's the same yesterday, today, and forever. That means that His commands haven't changed either, and neither has the reason why He gave them to us in the first place. And if you ask me, we need them more now in this world that we live in than ever before.

Let me try to explain how relevant they can be:

Command One: Exodus 20:3, *"You shall have no other gods before me."* When one hears the word "gods," it can be confusing and overlooked because we think of the pagan gods of stone, wood, or metal. Some were large and some were small, depending where one wanted to put them. So you bypass that one because, of course, you are not guilty of having a pagan god around. May I just simply say, BALONEY! I want you to know that gods do not have to be in the form of a statue. They can be yourself, your family, your home, your car, your addiction—ANYTHING or ANYONE you think you cannot live without. If you have ever even thought, "I could never live without...." GUILTY! You have a god. God starts with this command where we would expect because it really checks out our relationship with Him. And of course, don't lose sight of the implied message herein—we are to worship Him first and foremost.

Guilt—today people don't want to learn from it. Rather, they drown it in alcohol, escape it through entertainment, talk about it to a therapist, blame it on someone else, or suppress it through mental gymnastics, but it doesn't go away. It's like a stain in a fabric—the only thing that can wash away our sins is nothing but the blood of Jesus.

It is such an important command that He makes it more specific in the second one, Command Two: Exodus 20:4-6:

> *"You shall not make for yourself an idol in the form of anything in heaven above or on the earth beneath or in the waters below. You shall not bow down to them or worship them; for I, the LORD your God, am a jealous God, punishing the children for the sin of the fathers to the third and fourth generation of those who hate me, but showing love to a thousand generations of those who love me and keep my commandments."*

It's like He says it again to make sure that you know He means business. When we place Him in His proper place in our lives, we will stay on the right track on this journey of life on which He has placed us. He says this over and over to the people of Israel and to US. He will punish those who disobey and show His love to those who obey. He says He's a jealous God. He admits it! He will not share God-ship with anyone or anything else. He put's it in a way that NO one can miss His meaning. If you did not hear it here, you just plugged your spiritual ears. We are so good at choosing what we want to hear and then putting our fingers to those ears of ours to shut out what we really need to hear. That gesture reminds me of a little kid—rather childish, wouldn't you say? When are we going to learn that when God speaks, we need to listen, because He loves us and wants us living the most fulfilled, contented, joyful, and best life that He can and will make possible. John 4:23 reminds us:

> *"Yet a time is coming and has now come when the true worshipers will worship the Father in spirit*

and truth, for they are the kind of worshipers the Father seeks."

Command Three: Exodus 20:7, *"You shall not misuse the name of the LORD your God, for the LORD will not hold anyone guiltless who misuses his name."*

He commands that we never take His name in vain or misuse His name. You may be thinking that you do not have a problem with this one because you do not cuss. Nor do I. So for a long time I did not think I had a problem with this command because I take what comes out of my mouth very seriously. Believe me, I am far from perfect, but I am learning that my mouth is a direct reflection of my heart. *"You brood of vipers, how can you who are evil say anything good? For out of the overflow of the heart the mouth speaks"* (Matthew 12:34).

That's why this command is so important, and by the way, it's not just about cussing. What's in my heart determines who I keep company with, where I go, and what I say and do. I wear His name. I am going to say that again. I wear His name. That means, where I go, He goes. Who I am with, He's with. What I say and do, He's hearing and watching. I represent Him. So what does His name look like in our conversations, in the places we go or the people we're with? Would He be pleased? Would He be proud to be along or listening to what we're saying? Shouldn't our desire or goal be to please Him? It's something to think about. Isaiah prophesied that His name would be called, *Wonderful Counselor, Mighty God, Everlasting Father, Prince of Peace* (Isaiah 9:6b). The apostle Paul said that His name is *the name that is above every name* (Philippians 2:9). And to think that you and I claim to "wear that name." If that's the case, then that carries a big responsibility, but it's also a great honor. Don't misuse His name!

Command Four: Exodus 20:8,*"Remember the Sabbath day by keeping it holy."* Some call it the Sabbath; others call it Sunday. I, myself, don't think He cares what day you make it; He just commands that you take one day and STOP. He commands it because He knows that whatever takes up the other six days pulls us in every direction; and there comes a time when it is necessary to come to a halt and renew, refocus, reenergize, revive, reinforce, and re-center on the only One who can do all things for us. He wants that time. He knows we need that time. Even the best of Christians, with the best of intentions, need to be turned around from the pull of the world's thinking so as to be recharged to resist the temptation to be caught in its trap. Actually, we need to be turned around from ourselves. This world messes us up; this Sabbath day provides us with the opportunity to clean up the mess. The Lord will show each and every one of us in very special ways how we can make this day His. But I remember one Sunday when I sang at a church for their children's ministry. One father dropped his child off and said, "I hope the preacher is short winded today, because we have our bathing suits on underneath our clothes; as soon as this service is over, we're out of here and headed to the beach." I don't want to be judgmental here, so I'm just telling you the true story and let you decide if that sounds like what the Lord meant with this command. Is this the attitude that He's looking for on His day? Then again, I have ladies who tell me that their Bible Study day (and I have them almost every day of the week) is their best Sabbath day. Their lives stop for the time, and it is ALL about Him. Then that attitude and behavior carries them over throughout the whole day. They see and hear Him in everything they do and everywhere they go because their spirits were re-nourished with their God and they are now ready to face their week.

Here God changes His focus from the appropriate worship and treatment to be given to Him to commandments that look to our respect for and treatment of other people.

Command Five: Exodus 20:12a, *"Honor your father and your mother."* This command makes it crystal clear. We are to literally honor and respect our father and mother. Maybe your parents have not been the kind of parents you would have longed for or that the Lord intended, but the command still stands. Maybe you think that it is impossible because of your situation. Ask the Lord to help you. You won't be sorry. But I like to think that this command also means to honor ALL those in authority over us. The command does not say that we have to agree with them or approve of their behavior; but again, He says honor them. Politically, it's so easy to badmouth or make fun of those we do not care for. But as Christians, we are commanded to respect them, their office, and their position. The apostle Paul put it quite clearly in his letter to the Romans; and believe me, the Romans and the Jews were not bosom buddies. In chapter 13:1-7:

> *1Everyone must submit himself to the governing authorities, for there is no authority except that which God has established. The authorities that exist have been established by God. 2Consequently, he who rebels against the authority is rebelling against what God has instituted, and those who do so will bring judgment on themselves. 3For rulers hold no terror for those who do right, but for those who do wrong. Do you want to be free from fear of the one in authority? Then do what is right and he will commend you. 4For he is God's servant to do you good. But if you do wrong, be afraid, for he does not bear the sword for nothing. He is God's servant, an agent of wrath to bring punishment on the wrongdoer. 5Therefore, it is necessary to submit to the authorities, not only because of possible punishment but also because of conscience.*
>
> *6This is also why you pay taxes, for the authorities are God's servants, who give their full time to governing. 7Give everyone what you owe him: If you owe taxes, pay taxes; if revenue, then revenue; if respect, then respect; if honor, then honor.*

As part of our responsibility, we pray and then vote for a candidate we feel is the one who will do their job to the best of their ability, seeking God's help to do it. But then, what if the opponent wins? What went wrong? We panic. Remember, God is still on the throne! He is still the Master and blessed controller of all things. Sometimes it's hard for us to fathom, but God knows the exact person who should be in that position for His purpose. God is the Director of every span in time (past, present, and future), and He is directing this world's path to get it ready for His Son's return. I heard Anne Graham say once, "This world isn't falling apart, it's just falling into place." Take comfort in the truth of those words. The Lord does know what He's doing.

Command Six: Exodus 20:13, *"You shall not murder."* We think we can bypass this one for sure. It's a no-brainer. I dare say that 99.9% of those of you reading this have never actually, literally, murdered someone. WHOA! Wait a minute. Unless you are perfect, you have. Maybe you haven't killed a body, but have you killed a person's spirit by either your actions or words? If you've killed a relationship, killed a family's harmony, or killed a church's spiritual fellowship and well-being—you have murdered. God commands us to watch our tongue and emotions through the ways we utilize anger, hatred, slander, gossip, or failing to forgive.

> *"You have heard that it was said to the people long ago, `Do not murder, and anyone who murders will be subject to judgment.' But I tell you that anyone who is angry with his brother will be subject to judgment. Again, anyone who says to his brother, `Raca,' is answerable to the Sanhedrin. But anyone who says, `You fool!' will be in danger of the fire of hell."* (Matthew 5:21-22.)

Holding on to that grudge may be something you have convinced yourself you are entitled to after what someone did to you. Well, you're NOT, and He commands you not to murder someone's spirit. Killing destroys.

Command Seven: Exodus 20:14, *"You shall not commit adultery."* God created sex, and He thought it was a great idea. I'm coming right out and calling it for what it is. But He also knew that this creation could be a real rascal. So He created sex for within the fence of marriage and the marriage of one man and one woman.

(Genesis 2:24.)   But, Jesus explained it even further in Matthew 5:27-28:

"You have heard that it was said, 'Do not commit adultery.' But I tell you that anyone who looks at a woman lustfully has already committed adultery with her in his heart."

The apostle Paul says in his letter to the Philippians in chapter 4:8:

Finally, brothers, whatever is true, whatever is noble, whatever is right, whatever is pure, whatever is lovely, whatever is admirable—if anything is excellent or praiseworthy—think about such things.

Paul also says in Romans 12:2a:

Do not conform any longer to the pattern of this world, but be transformed by the renewing of your mind.

Adultery starts in the mind and heart first. But if this thought is taken captive by the Lord Jesus, it will never come out in an action. God knew that our jumping the fence with this one would horribly hurt so many people. And it has such lasting consequences—especially on innocent children, and you know how much our Lord loves children.

He called a little child and had him stand among them. And he said: "I tell you the truth, unless you change and become like little children, you will never enter the kingdom of heaven. Therefore, whoever humbles himself like this child is the greatest in the kingdom of heaven.
"And whoever welcomes a little child like this in my name welcomes me. But if anyone causes one of these little ones who believe in me to sin, it

*would be better for him to have a large millstone
hung around his neck and to be drowned in the
depths of the sea"* (Matthew 18:2-6).

So, yes, sex is a great creation. But use great caution. Listen
to His command. It will save a ton of heartache.

Command eight: Exodus 20:15, *"You shall not steal."* This
does not just mean robbing a bank, jewelry store, or your nearest
mini-mart. He's talking about: from your employer by wasting time
or not giving your best, owning a business and overcharging or
selling an inferior product for normal cost, borrowing and not paying
back, indulging ourselves and letting others go hungry, cheating on
our taxes, etc. We even steal from God when we fail to worship Him
and keep our daily appointments with Him, and instead, put our own
personal concerns ahead of His. I think this one is an easy one to
fail, but it is also an easy one to understand and to do something
about. It's not a choice. It's a command.

Command nine: Exodus 20:16, *"You shall not give false
testimony against your neighbor."* This one has so many "feelers."
The obvious is that we do not lie about someone. But that also
means not stretching the truth, exaggerating, or tearing someone
down to make yourself look better. Like stabbing someone in the
back—saying one thing to their face and then saying the opposite
behind their back. This command also deals with our tongue-trouble.
Listen to James in chapter 1:26, *If anyone considers himself religious
and yet does not keep a tight rein on his tongue, he deceives himself
and his religion is worthless.*

Also in chapter 3:3-8:

> *When we put bits into the mouths of horses
> to make them obey us, we can turn the whole
> animal. Or take ships as an example. Although they
> are so large and are driven by strong winds, they
> are steered by a very small rudder wherever the
> pilot wants to go. Likewise the tongue is a small*

*part of the body, but it makes great boasts. Consider
what a great forest is set on fire by a small spark.
The tongue also is a fire, a world of evil among the
parts of the body. It corrupts the whole person, sets
the whole course of his life on fire, and is itself set
on fire by hell.*

*All kinds of animals, birds, reptiles and
creatures of the sea are being tamed and have been
tamed by man, but no man can tame the tongue. It is
a restless evil, full of deadly poison.*

From Jesus' great Sermon on the Mount in Matthew 5-7, one
of His many important points was, *"Simply let your `Yes' be `Yes,'
and your `No,' `No'..."* (5:37a). God wants His people to be those
who can be counted on. He wants us trustworthy and dependable.
That in turn is a good testimony to Him and about Him. So keep
what comes out of your mouth within the fence.

Command ten: Exodus 20:17a, *"You shall not covet."* This
one affects us all on the subject of materialism. God knew our
roaming eyes would look at others and want what they have. This
one when outside of the fence has gotten so bad that our world
judges people's worth by what they have. Thus comes jealousy,
gambling, debt, and out-of-control charge card accounts. God knew
that covetous humans outside the fence would be singing the worldly
song, "I want, I want, I want," and as it just keeps repeating itself, the
more trapped they become.

There was a popular secular saying a few years back:
"Whoever winds up with the most toys in the end wins!" Sad isn't
it? As Christians we know:

*"Do not store up for yourselves treasures
on earth, where moth and rust destroy, and where
thieves break in and steal. But store up for
yourselves treasures in heaven, where moth and
rust do not destroy, and where thieves do not break
in and steal. For where your treasure is, there your
heart will be also.*

*"The eye is the lamp of the body. If your
eyes are good, your whole body will be full of light.
But if your eyes are bad, your whole body will be
full of darkness. If then the light within you is
darkness, how great is that darkness!*

*"No one can serve two masters. Either he
will hate the one and love the other, or he will be
devoted to the one and despise the other. You
cannot serve both God and Money."*
(Matthew 6:19-24.)

True contentment and satisfaction is possible, but never in anything of this world—only in Jesus.

These commands ✝ were given to us because He loves us. Don't ever forget that. He just wants to keep those He loves from hurting Him, themselves, and others. He wants us to stay out of trouble so that we do not have to suffer the consequences. He wants us living the abundant life, and that's only found within the fence. It's a great way to go to bed at night, knowing that you have a clear conscience and are able to get up in the morning ready to start the day with confidence, and knowing that He will be right there with you. When you have a healthy, holy, fear of your God, you will think twice for sure about jumping that fence.

In a sermon that was preached in our church, I heard a story that really helped me understand that when God fences us in, it actually is an act of life-changing freedom.

*But the man who looks intently into the perfect law
that gives freedom, and continues to do this, not
forgetting what he has heard, but doing it—he will
be blessed in what he does* (James 1:25).

To some it looks like boundaries that are confining—a prison that keeps you from being who you want to be and doing what you want to do. There were two brothers. One brother listened to the instruction of his parents and learned from their faith, which led to his personal faith in God Almighty. He lived within the fence and obeyed the rules, and he saw how the Lord could use him for His service. He found life to be full and satisfying. The other brother did not want to stay within the fence. He didn't want anyone telling him what to do. He wasn't going to be bound by rules. One day, because of all his addictions, he burned down his house with his wife in it. His wife managed to get out safely, but the house burned to the ground, and she called the police. Now every week, on the same day, at the same time, the one brother visits the other one; one in everyday clothes of his choosing, the other one behind glass in orange prison clothes. The question is: which brother is the free one? God knows us so well. His Truth sets us free. Now I understand what that means. If you want to live in real freedom, here are four solid fence posts that are guaranteed to keep you within the fence:

1. The fact that He is God and you are not.
2. The Bible is God's Word, and every word is the absolute Truth.
3. Pursue Truth given by God and not man's opinion.
4. Practice your faith. Obey His Word and live by it completely.

Those are rock solid fence posts that will set you free and keep you living free! What a great way to live!

CHAPTER 5

JESUS'  SIGNPOSTS

"The Water": ✝ Pg. 105

● ...John 4:10-14, *Jesus answered her, "If you knew the gift of God and who it is that asks you for a drink, you would have asked him and he would have given you living water." "Sir," the woman said, "you have nothing to draw with and the well is deep. Where can you get this living water? Are you greater than our father Jacob, who gave us the well and drank from it himself, as did also his sons and his flocks and herds?" Jesus answered, "Everyone who drinks this water will be thirsty again,* **but whoever drinks the water I give him will never thirst. Indeed, the water I give him will become in him a spring of water welling up to eternal life."**

"Manna (Bread)": ✝ Pg. 106

● ...John 6:31-35, *Our forefathers ate the manna in the desert; as it is written: `He gave them bread from heaven to eat.'" Jesus said to them, "I tell you the truth, it is not Moses who has given you the bread from heaven, but it is my Father who gives you the true bread from heaven. For the bread of God is he who comes down from heaven and gives life to the world." "Sir," they said, "from now on give us this bread."*

Then Jesus declared, "I am the bread of life. He who comes to me will never go hungry, and he who believes in me will never be thirsty.

"These Commands": ✟ Pg. 118

●...Matthew 5:17-18, *"Do not think that I* [Jesus] *have come to abolish the Law or the Prophets;* ___I have not come to abolish them but to fulfill them.___ *I tell you the truth, until heaven and earth disappear, not the smallest letter, not the least stroke of a pen, will by any means disappear from the Law until everything is accomplished."*

Lesson 5: Grumblers Need Commands
Exodus 15:22 - Exodus 20

1. What was the mood of the Israelites only three days after the time of glorious praise? Why?

2. Why do problems cause such mood swings? Should they? Why not? (What is the root problem in this question?)

3. Now what were the Israelites grumbling about? (15:23.)

4. What does grumbling do to your facial countenance and your entire attitude? Does this attract anyone to you and make them want to be around you?

5. God made a decree with Israel in 15:26. What is the little, yet HUGE word in this verse? Why? What is God's point here? Is this principle hard to understand? Hard to do? Why?

6. God is faithful, unconditionally loving, and patient (thank goodness). How does He supply for you? What do you know about the promise of God supplying your needs? Philippians 4:19.

7. What did some people do with God's instructions? (16:20, 27.) Should you have been surprised with the consequences? Is there a life lesson here?

8. Why should you be appalled with Israel's question in 17:7? But, have you ever asked that same question? If you have, who moved?

9.   Go through each commandment and state what it says and
        what it means for you today.

10.   What does command mean?   Why did God give
        commandments? Is that something that you should think
        about for awhile?

11.   What does true freedom mean?

12.   What are the solid fence posts that will keep you living free?

6

How Could They Do That?

When Moses went up to the top of Mount Sinai to receive the Law of God, the experience took awhile—forty days and forty nights to be exact. Now granted, that is long, but not THAT long; and I am almost certain that when he put his brother Aaron in charge, he thought the people were in good hands. (Aaron, Moses' brother, had been his right hand man. He was years older than Moses, and was the priest of that nation.) Moses knew that he had to concentrate on what God was giving him. Those Laws of God would be followed for generations, and he wanted to make sure he received every detail. Unfortunately, the Israelites were not in good hands. Aaron was a pushover. When the "natives" got restless, they went to Aaron with a demand:

> *"Come, make us gods who will go before us. As for*
> *this fellow Moses who brought us up out of Egypt,*
> *we don't know what has happened to him"*
> (Exodus 32:1b).

It had only been 40 days; and it was Moses, backed by God, who had faced Pharaoh for them, had led them through the Red Sea, and had gone to the Lord for food and water on their behalf. And now they are calling him, "this FELLOW Moses"? Oh, do they ever have a little bit of Egypt still inside of them! Does the phrase, "How soon we forget" come to mind?

Instead of standing up to them and symbolically knocking their blocks off, Aaron gave in to their demands and told them to bring to him all their gold earrings. Read 32:4a, *He took what they handed him and made it into an idol cast in the shape of a calf, fashioning it with a tool.*

Now, remember that verse for just a little later. In verses 5-6:

When Aaron saw this, he built an altar in front of the calf and announced, "Tomorrow there will be a festival to the LORD." So the next day the people rose early and sacrificed burnt offerings and presented fellowship offerings. Afterward they sat down to eat and drink and got up to indulge in revelry.

DISGUSTING! Oh, I'm not going to deny that sin can have its fun and laughs, but the consequences are never funny. Sin is NEVER worth it.

If we claim to be without sin, we deceive ourselves and the truth is not in us. If we confess our sins, he is faithful and just and will forgive us our sins and purify us from all unrighteousness. If we claim we have not sinned, we make him out to be a liar and his word has no place in our lives (1 John 1:8-10).

When picking the shape of an idol, did you ever wonder why they chose a COW of all things? But if you remember, during the plagues God used one of the plagues to kill the Egyptians' livestock because the bull was sacred and worshiped by them. That's why you can tell that the Israelites did not yet have all of Egypt out of their system. Worshiping a cow! Isn't that totally ridiculous when you look at that scene from "inside the fence"?

When the long forty days and forty nights came to an end, and the Law had been written by the very finger of God on tablets of stone, Moses started down the mountain carrying those precious Words. He probably was very much looking forward to seeing his people and sharing with them this astounding experience. But instead, he saw them worshiping this golden calf! I can honestly say I am CERTAIN he could not believe what he saw! In fact, he got so mad that he took those tablets and threw them down in fury, and they broke into pieces. He then took the calf they had made and burned it in the fire. Then he ground it to powder, scattered it on the water, and made the Israelites drink it. Then he went to Aaron and asked him, *"What did these people do to you, that you led them into such great sin?"* (v. 21b.)

He basically made Aaron responsible. Aaron was not the leader Moses thought he would be. Leadership sounds so powerful and exciting. This world places leaders in the inevitable position of being above others. The Lord says that true leadership is being willing to serve—just the opposite of the world's definition. The Lord wants ALL leaders to rely on the guidance of the One and only Leader—willing to serve Him and follow His directions because His directions will never lead to the wrong destination. When you are given the responsibility of leadership, that means you have followers. They are trusting their leader. That's why Jesus said that to whom much is given, much will be required. (See Luke 12:48.) I love teaching Bible Study to hundreds of ladies. But it is an enormous responsibility. They trust me. I never want to lead them in the wrong direction with MY opinion. That's why, as a leader, I must go to MY Leader to make very sure that what they receive is from Him and not just a bunch of facts sprinkled with my lame interpretations.

Aaron's answer, if not so serious, would be hysterical. Verses 22-24 tell us that Aaron said:

> *"Do not be angry, my lord," Aaron answered. "You know how prone these people are to evil. They said to me, 'Make us gods who will go before us. As for this fellow Moses who brought us up out of Egypt, we don't know what has happened to him.' So I told them, 'Whoever has any gold jewelry, take it off.' Then they gave me the gold, and I threw it into the fire, and out came this calf!"*

What? Out came a calf?

I asked you to remember what the Bible said in verse 4 about how Aaron MADE it into a calf by using a tool. Aaron, you are BUSTED! But what Moses was most disappointed about was the kind of testimony this was to their enemies. When we sin, we don't always sin alone, and then it is witnessed by others. No wonder God commanded us NOT to misuse His name in the Ten Commandments. What a mockery and joke we can make of our gracious Lord by our behavior!

Moses went to the Lord and begged His forgiveness. In fact, he even offered not only to give his life in exchange for the Israelites' forgiveness, but also his eternal life. ✞ He offered to allow the Lord to blot out his name from God's book of life. The Lord answered him by saying that it doesn't work that way. Everyone is responsible for his or her own choices and will have to suffer the consequences. As I write this, though, I am so taken with the message of the gospel right now. The whole purpose of the Old Testament was to show that we had our choice. We chose sin, and we should be suffering the punishment deserved: death and HELL. But instead we are offered grace—undeserved favor. Jesus took our punishment. I heard once that grace is getting what we DON'T deserve and NOT getting what we do deserve. But like the apostle Paul says in Romans 6:1-2, *What shall we say, then? Shall we go on sinning so that grace may increase? By no means! We died to sin; how can we live in it any longer?*

You never like to hurt the one you love, and sin hurts Him. Why would we want to do that?

You might not readily pick up the theme of God's "grace" in the Old Testament, but you see the results of it time and time again. In chapter 34, the Lord gave Moses the Law again, but it came along with this warning in Exodus 34:1-7:

> *1 The LORD said to Moses, "Chisel out two stone tablets like the first ones, and I will write on them the words that were on the first tablets, which you broke. 2Be ready in the morning, and then come up on Mount Sinai. Present yourself to me there on top of the mountain. 3No one is to come with you or be seen anywhere on the mountain; not even the flocks and herds may graze in front of the mountain."*
>
> *4So Moses chiseled out two stone tablets like the first ones and went up Mount Sinai early in the morning, as the LORD had commanded him;*

and he carried the two stone tablets in his hands.
5Then the LORD came down in the cloud and stood
there with him and proclaimed his name, the LORD.
6And he passed in front of Moses, proclaiming,
"The LORD, the LORD, the compassionate and
gracious God, slow to anger, abounding in love and
faithfulness, 7maintaining love to thousands, and
forgiving wickedness, rebellion and sin. Yet he does
not leave the guilty unpunished; he punishes the
children and their children for the sin of the fathers
to the third and fourth generation."

When Moses came down from the mountain this time, Aaron and all the Israelites saw Moses, and his face was radiant. Psalm 34:5 says, *Those who look to him are radiant; their faces are never covered with shame.*

When one has a personal, close, intimate relationship with the Lord, it shows. Somehow, it just shows. When Christ changes a life, it comes out in our countenance—our face. It's hard to explain. All I know is that it does. Let me give you a personal illustration. My husband Tom and I have friends who were once in NASCAR auto racing. He was one of the drivers. We became friends with them through Bible Study. Because the study affected their lives so much, they asked if they could put "Lynnelle Pierce Ministries" on one of the back corners of their race cars. Because we were not race car fans at the time, I have to admit I wasn't too sure whether that was a good idea. I know now that it was a high compliment, but at the time I was concerned what my name would be next to. I didn't know them very well at the time. So I prayed about it, and it took a split second for the Holy Spirit to reveal a verse I had learned.

Then Jesus came to them and said, "All authority in
heaven and on earth has been given to me.
Therefore go and make disciples of all nations,
baptizing them in the name of the Father and of the
Son and of the Holy Spirit, and teaching them to
obey everything I have commanded you. And surely

I am with you always, to the very end of the age"
(Matthew 28:18-20).

That verse was a command of Jesus Himself, and that was
for us to go into all the world and bring this life-changing gospel.
How are they going to hear if no one tells them? How are they going
to know Him unless someone shares Him? So, I said, "Yes, I would
be honored." The rest I left in the Lord's hands.

Well, come February, they invited us to see the car with the
logo on the back at the Daytona 500. What a way to be introduced to
NASCAR! Might as well start at the top! When we were given the
proper passes to get in the garage and in the pits, we felt we had just
been ushered into a whole new world. They took us to the track and
told us to take a look. There it was, the race car with "Lynnelle
Pierce Ministries" going around the Daytona 500 track. It took my
breath away. It was beautiful. I was thrilled to say the least. The car
was brought to the garage and then back on the track many times that
week, and Tom and I would go through check points constantly for
safety reasons. The same police officer seemed to be at this check
point all week. Every time I walked through, I would show him my
pass and say hello.

One night Tom and I were standing by the fence in the pit
area where the cars go in and out of the garage, and I felt a tug on my
arm. I turned around, and there stood that police officer. I was a
little nervous at first, thinking maybe I wasn't where I was supposed
to be. But quickly he said this, "Ma'am, I have been watching you all
week. I don't know who you are or where you have come from, but I
just felt that I needed to come to you because you would understand.
I lost my son, his future wife, and her parents because of carbon
monoxide poisoning. I cannot seem to shake the pain. It's been two
years, and the battle still rages within me." Think about it. There
were literally thousands of people that this man saw on a daily basis.
All he knew was that I was a part of a race team, but I could have
been one of the mechanics for all he knew (well, maybe not a
mechanic). So that means he never heard me sing. He never heard
me teach a Bible Study. He didn't even know my name. Why did he
pick me? There is a simple reason: it's because Jesus shows up on
our faces when He lives and has control of our lives.

Most of the time when people are searching for answers, they don't know it, but what they need is Jesus. And I do mean to be so simple and blunt that Jesus is who everyone needs. The only thing I could do for this police officer was admit to him that I did not have the power to take away his pain, but I knew of SOMEONE who could, if he was interested. He was. And at the Daytona race track, at a night race, I stood there with my arm around this police officer praying for him. Don't kid yourself. It shows on your face when you love Jesus, when your relationship is real.

I heard a sermon* once about two different kinds of Christians. One is a "cultural Christian": he or she will pick and chose from the Christian faith what they WANT. When it fits. When they need something. Then there is the "practicing Christian": he or she is all in for Jesus. He IS his or her life. In good times and bad, these kinds of Christians know their God is up to something for their good and believe that He has promised the kind of life no one else can give. They take the time to learn from Him through prayer and His Word. They desire to obey His commands and choose to live a healthy life. They are also willing to meet with Him through times of communion, prayer, Christian fellowship and conversation, hospitality, forgiveness, and reconciliation. A life like that can only make you radiate with His splendor, and I know it must show because I have NO other explanation. But then, the Bible did say we would, didn't it?

Moses wrote the book of Leviticus to specifically explain the Law. He wrote the book of Numbers as a continuation of Exodus, and Deuteronomy as a summary or recap of events. As we move into the book of Numbers, the Israelites had left Mount Sinai; and after this journey they had some down time. Maybe it even got boring, and there was nothing to do as they had to stop and stay in a place for whatever reason. I know that when Tom and I would be on a singing tour, the actual concerts were wonderful, but the down time in between concerts was the worst part. I think that in Numbers 12, Aaron and Miriam were in one of the down times. It was just the two of them, and they got to talking—not really just talking, they were complaining and being mean spirited. Oh, they thought it was only the two of them. No one else was around, and they just needed to vent. They had to get this off their chests (sound too familiar?).

They didn't like Moses' wife, plus they weren't getting any attention. After all, they had worked just as hard as Moses, and he was getting all the accolades. The thing is, they found out someone did overhear their conversation. We should remember this when we feel we are having a private one-on-one conversation out of others' hearing. Listen to Psalm 139:1-4:

> *O LORD, you have searched me and you know me.*
> *You know when I sit and when I rise; you perceive*
> *my thoughts from afar.*
> *You discern my going out and my lying down; you*
> *are familiar with all my ways.*
> *Before a word is on my tongue you know it*
> *completely, O LORD.*

Guess who's listening to every word of our conversation? The Lord is always there.

In Numbers 12:9, it says, *The anger of the LORD burned against them, and he left them.* What's wrong with a little venting, or a little gossip, or a bit of a negative spirit, we wonder? Well, the Lord detests it as much as He detests murder and adultery.

> *There are six things the LORD hates, seven that are*
> *detestable to him:*
> *haughty eyes, a lying tongue, hands that shed innocent*
> *blood,*
> *a heart that devises wicked schemes, feet that are quick to*
> *rush into evil,*
> *a false witness who pours out lies and a man who stirs up*
> *dissension among brothers* (Proverbs 6:16-19).

The Lord called a family meeting. Poor Moses didn't deserve any of their nonsense, because the Lord revealed that *(Moses was a very humble man, more humble than anyone else on the face of the earth.)* (Numbers 12:3.) As a result of her conversation with Aaron, Miriam was smitten with leprosy and was confined outside the camp for seven days. Instead of being angry and holding a grudge, Moses begged the Lord to heal her. This really showed the character of Moses. I am sure that what was supposed to have been a quiet conversation just between the two of them now spread like wildfire among the million people. Scary, isn't it, when you think about some of the "conversations" you have had?

Do you ever wonder how come Aaron wasn't punished? I think he was. Have you ever watched someone "get it" and you know that you were just as guilty? I believe that by watching his sister suffer, it was indeed punishment—maybe even worse than hers.

In this story of Miriam and Aaron, I couldn't help but think of the difference between criticism and correcting. Now, we all need to be corrected. Correcting is when you have the other person's best interest in mind. I have three people in my life who I have given permission to correct me. One sees me all the time, one sees me now and then, and the other doesn't see me very often. I chose them specifically because I know that they love me and want the best for me and the ministry the Lord has given to me. We need people to be watching, because sometimes we can drift off the path without even realizing it ourselves; and it may take someone who loves us to bring it to the forefront so it can be dealt with. Criticism is when you have your best interest in mind. You are just plain crabby or out of sorts, and you choose to be critical or find fault with someone else so that you don't have to see the ugly in you. And that's wrong. The Lord will call you on it, for sure.

Now Aaron and Miriam were wonderful, godly, spiritual people. So if THEY can fall into a trap like that, we all can. Never put your life in cruise mode regarding your godliness and church going. Stay in your Bible. Stay in prayer. Stay connected to your God. If we disconnect from Him, that means we think we can handle it on our own; and I believe Aaron and Miriam showed us what can happen to any one of us at any time.

We all crave attention now and then. If we work hard but do not get the thanks and appreciation we think we deserve, we might find ourselves in the same ugly place in which Miriam and Aaron found themselves. We too, then, are guilty of putting someone else down so that we look better. (Some of us think it, and some will actually say it.) I heard this story that might help. There was this missionary coming home to the states after serving the Lord in Africa for 25 years. On the same ship, coming home from a three-week safari, was President Roosevelt. When the ship arrived, banners were waving and confetti was falling. The bands were playing, and the crowd was shouting with excitement to see the President returning home from Africa. The poor missionary could hardly get through all the pomp and circumstance to find someone to take him to his destination. He found himself feeling quite discouraged. In fact, he even asked the Lord how come the President got all that attention when he came home from a pleasure trip, but after he had served with his whole heart for 25 years, he got no attention at all. In his spirit, he could hear the Lord's gentle Voice saying, "But, my son, you're not Home yet." May we seek nothing from this world!

> *"Be careful not to do your `acts of righteousness' before men, to be seen by them. If you do, you will have no reward from your Father in heaven.*
> *"So when you give to the needy, do not announce it with trumpets, as the hypocrites do in the synagogues and on the streets, to be honored by men. I tell you the truth, they have received their reward in full"* (Matthew 6:1-2).

May our goal be to hear the words from our Lord Himself, *"`Well done, good and faithful servant!'"* (Matthew 25:21a.) In our attention seeking world, may we know that our mission isn't to please man, but to please the God who loves us and saved us. That should be enough.

The Israelites continued to grumble, complain, and doubt. Listen to the words from Numbers 14:18a, *"The LORD is slow to anger, abounding in love and forgiving sin and rebellion. Yet he does not leave the guilty unpunished.'"*

The Lord had had it! What should have been a journey of weeks turned into one that spanned over a period of 40 years. Desert time for 40 years would teach them that God is serious. The reason for 40 years? Well, I'll let the Bible tell you.

26The LORD said to Moses and Aaron: 27"How long will this wicked community grumble against me? I have heard the complaints of these grumbling Israelites. 28So tell them, `As surely as I live, declares the LORD, I will do to you the very things I heard you say: 29In this desert your bodies will fall—every one of you twenty years old or more who was counted in the census and who has grumbled against me. 30Not one of you will enter the land I swore with uplifted hand to make your home, except Caleb son of Jephunneh and Joshua son of Nun. 31As for your children that you said would be taken as plunder, I will bring them in to enjoy the land you have rejected. 32But you—your bodies will fall in this desert. 33Your children will be shepherds here for forty years, suffering for your unfaithfulness, until the last of your bodies lies in the desert. 34For forty years—one year for each of the forty days you explored the land—you will suffer for your sins and know what it is like to have me against you.' 35I, the LORD, have spoken, and I will surely do these things to this whole wicked community, which has banded together against me. They will meet their end in this desert; here they will die."
(Numbers 14:26-35).

It's hard to end a chapter on that note, but sometimes it's necessary. God hates disobedience. Disobedience needs to be corrected. God does have our best interest in mind. He will discipline those He loves; and remember, He loves us all. We have to learn, and like my dad would tell me when I was a little girl and disobeyed, I think God says the same to us today, "This hurts me more than it does you, but I love you and you have to learn." SMACK!

There's not much to tell about during those 40 years. What would there be to tell from walking in circles for that long. But after 40 years, a new generation had begun. You would think they would have a new slate, that they had turned over a new leaf. But in Numbers 20:2-5, listen to this:

> *Now there was no water for the community, and the people gathered in opposition to Moses and Aaron. They quarreled with Moses and said, "If only we had died when our brothers fell dead before the LORD! Why did you bring the LORD's community into this desert, that we and our livestock should die here? Why did you bring us up out of Egypt to this terrible place? It has no grain or figs, grapevines or pomegranates. And there is no water to drink!"*

Attitudes carry down through family lines. Children do notice. Yes, they see and hear, and they also catch our attitudes. Hadn't they heard how the Lord provided for their families' every need, and the only reason their families had been in the desert was not GOD'S fault? Moses and Aaron were exasperated! They went to the Lord and fell facedown. They were at their wits end. In Numbers 20: 8-9:

> *"Take the staff, and you and your brother Aaron gather the assembly together. Speak to that rock before their eyes and it will pour out its water. You will bring water out of the rock for the community so they and their livestock can drink."* ✝

The story continues. *So Moses took the staff from the LORD's presence, just as he commanded him.* Moses took his staff, and he got the whole assembly together so that they could witness God's provision again. But Moses was so angry that instead of speaking to the rock as he was told to do, he struck it. Not once, but twice. Water did gush out, and the community drank, as did their livestock. All seemed fine. It wasn't! Listen to verse 12:

> *But the LORD said to Moses and Aaron, "Because you did not trust in me enough to honor me as holy*

in the sight of the Israelites, you will not bring this
community into the land I give them."

What? After 80 years of preparation, and 40 years with these
stiff-necked whiners and cry babies, Moses can't finish the job?

I dare say we can all empathize with Moses. We have had
people or circumstances drive us to the point of craziness. Then,
after what comes out of either our mouths or our actions, we
generally wish we could have a do-over.

I remember when our son Jason was a first grader (he is a
grown man now with boys of his own). He was such a cutie, but one
day that little boy became so exasperated that he got himself into
some trouble. You see, I have been in the public eye for many years,
and my poor boys have had to deal with that. Now sometimes it
could be a wonderful perk, but there were also times when they
suffered. One day while riding the school bus, a bully of a kid just
kept hammering him on how his mom was "for the birds." Now,
granted, Jason knew better, but this kid brought him to his breaking
point, so Jason hauled off and punched him in the face! When I first
heard about it, I secretly wanted to hug him for defending me. But,
of course, I had to talk to him about the seriousness of letting our
emotions get out of control and causing us to act out in ways that are
not appropriate or are downright wrong. Fortunately for Jason, the
damage was not too severe, and his consequences not too painful; but
nonetheless, it certainly shows that out-of-control anger begins at a
very early age. Kids do not have to be taught how to react
inappropriately when they get mad, that's for sure! It is just another
sign of our natural sinful nature. Learning how to control anger has
to be taught and put into practice. And that lesson needs to be in
action continuously until we leave this earth, because that's just the
way life is—full of people and moments that can drive us to a point
beyond control.

God means business—even with Moses. As humble of a
servant as Moses had been, he was just human, and he had one major
flaw that he battled during his life. That was anger. If there had
been anger management classes back then, Moses would have been
sent to one. Remember when he saw one of the Egyptians beating an
Israelite back when he was 40? He killed the guy! When he came

down the mountain and saw the Israelites worshiping the golden calf, he smashed the tablets. Now, when God told him to <u>speak</u> to the rock, he <u>struck</u> it <u>twice</u>. Anger is a very strong emotion, and when it gets out of control, it's very damaging. You have probably heard of righteous anger. Be careful with that. It can turn on a dime. God has righteous anger. He gets angry at sin, but God is NEVER out of control. Moses had righteous anger when he saw what the Egyptians and the Israelites had done in their sinning, but he let that anger get the best of him, and then he lost control.   James says in chapter 1:19-20:

> *My dear brothers, take note of this: Everyone should be quick to listen, slow to speak and slow to become angry, for man's anger does not bring about the righteous life that God desires.*

We can be very angry at the sin, but we need to watch out that our behavior never gets out of control. That's when we say or do something we later regret, and we can't take it back.

Moses admitted in Deuteronomy 3 that he pleaded with the Lord to recant. But the Lord came back and said no, and we are not going to talk about it again. Do you think that Moses would have given just about anything to have that past angry moment back? What about Adam and Eve? What about Peter when he denied Jesus, or Paul when he persecuted Christians? What about you? Do you have a few times you wish you could do a retake? You, like Moses and everyone else, will suffer the consequences of your sin. God can use those consequences for our good, though. Read what the writer of Hebrews says in chapter 12:7-11:

> *Endure hardship as discipline; God is treating you as sons. For what son is not disciplined by his father? If you are not disciplined (and everyone undergoes discipline), then you are illegitimate children and not true sons. Moreover, we have all had human fathers who disciplined us and we respected them for it. How much more should we submit to the Father of our spirits and live! Our fathers disciplined us for a little*

while as they thought best; but God disciplines us for our good, that we may share in his holiness. No discipline seems pleasant at the time, but painful. Later on, however, it produces a harvest of righteousness and peace for those who have been trained by it.

This has been a hard and painful chapter, but look how it ends. Even in discipline, God loves you. God loves you.

*The sermon illustration about "cultural" and "practicing" Christians on page 133 comes from a sermon given by:

REV. DAVID B. WARD, PHD
Associate Dean, School of Theology & Ministry
Director of Kern Ministry Program
Indiana Wesleyan University

CHAPTER 6

JESUS'   SIGNPOSTS

"Eternal Life": ✞ Pg. 130

Truly a life and death example here. Moses' offer of a personal sacrifice on behalf of the Israelites, while heartfelt, would not satisfy God's requirements. You see, God requires a perfect, sinless, sacrifice by the One who kept all of God's commandments. That is <u>Jesus</u> – not Moses. Don't miss the critical personal application here. You cannot stand in place for another's eternal destiny nor depend on another's for your own. Only Jesus can provide the pathway to the Father for all eternity!

● ...John 3:16, *"For God so loved the world that he gave his one and only Son, that whoever believes in him shall not perish but have eternal life.*

● ...John 14:6, *Jesus answered, "I am the way and the truth and the life. No one comes to the Father except through me.*

"Rock": ✞ Pg. 138

● ...1 Corinthians 10:3-4, *They all ate the same spiritual food and drank the same spiritual drink; for they drank from the spiritual rock that accompanied them, and that rock was Christ.*

Lesson 6: How Could They Do That?
Various Passages

1. From Exodus 20 - 31, what did God give to Moses on Mount Sinai? How long was he up there on the mountain?

2. In Exodus 32, relive the sad story of the Israelites. Why would they do such a thing? Why is it so much easier to worship or trust something you can see? But, what is faith? (Hebrews 11:1.) Why does faith please God?

3. How did Moses react as he came down from the mountain and saw the people's idol worship? What did he ask Aaron (who was responsible)? How did Aaron answer? What did God do? Is He serious about His commandment in Exodus 20:3-4?

4. What is the difference between a "cultural Christian? and a "practicing" one?

5. What is grace? How do you see it in Exodus 34:1-7?

6. When Moses came down the mountain the second time, what was his face like? (Ex. 34:29.) How can you radiate Christ? Is it noticeable to others?

7. What happened in Numbers 12?

8. Why does human nature crave attention? Who should you be aiming to please? Why?

9. What is the difference between criticizing and correcting?

10.   What does the Lord hear in all your conversations? (Psalm 139:1-4.)

11.   If this can happen to two godly people like Miriam and Aaron, what does this say to you? How can you stay on your guard to prevent this from happening?

12.   The Israelites continued to grumble and complain. How can you explain Numbers 14:18? Read the rest of Numbers 14 and see what God's punishment and discipline were. Who does God discipline and why? (Hebrews 12:7-11.)

13.   What happened in Numbers 20? What was Moses' flaw that he battled all his life? How did God discipline Moses? Why wasn't that punishment too harsh?

14.   What does James 1:19-20 say? Why would these verses be good to take note of?

7

Joshua

I don't think we can even imagine how difficult it was for Moses to sit on the cliff of rock and just LOOK at the Promised Land. It breaks my heart to think of that old man, who worked so hard and put up with so much, who now could only look at the land instead of entering it. But instead of indulging in self-pity, he wrote and recited a song to the Israelites in Deuteronomy 32. You know, that was a great idea! When words are put to music, have you noticed how that tune will come back to you over and over and the words just seem to flow out?

When I did a lot of singing for children, I remember a minister thanking me for teaching his little girls many lessons about the Fruit of the Spirit, the Lord's Prayer, and many other Bible truths. I made certain that when I recorded a project for children, it was totally filled with God's Word. When I teach Bible Study, a big part of the time (not as big a part as the Bible lesson, of course) is spent on singing. I spend a great deal of time picking out songs that will go with the lesson. And more often than not, we will also end the time with a song, because I know that tune and those words will keep ringing in their hearts and then out of their mouths long after they go home. Music is such a gift from God. It is such a wonderful way of expressing what is overflowing in our hearts. Oh, I know that Satan has gotten his grimy mitts on it, but God intended for it to be a sweet tool to keep His Word singing in our lives as we travel with Him hand-in-hand in this world.

When Moses finished, he said to the people in Deuteronomy 32:44-47:

> *Moses came with Joshua son of Nun and spoke all*
> *the words of this song in the hearing of the people.*
> *When Moses finished reciting all these words to all*
> *Israel, he said to them, "Take to heart all the words*
> *I have solemnly declared to you this day, so that you*
> *may command your children to obey carefully all*
> *the words of this law. They are not just idle words*
> *for you—they are your life. By them you will live*
> *long in the land you are crossing the Jordan to*
> *possess."* ✞

That is quite the statement. If your children mean ANYTHING to you at all, make sure they are taught the Word of God. His words are not just a bunch of mumble jumble, they are LIFE from the Life Giver. In other words, it will be worth your time to teach your kids the Truth of God. It will make a monumental difference in their lives.

In Deuteronomy 33-34, Moses blessed the Twelve Tribes of Israel, and then climbed Mount Nebo. In chapter 34:5-7 it says:

> *And Moses the servant of the LORD died there in*
> *Moab, as the LORD had said. He buried him in*
> *Moab, in the valley opposite Beth Peor, but to this*
> *day no one knows where his grave is. Moses was a*
> *hundred and twenty years old when he died, yet his*
> *eyes were not weak nor his strength gone.*

I know that we have spent a great amount of space and time on the life of Moses, but Scripture says:

> *Since then, no prophet has risen in Israel like*
> *Moses, whom the LORD knew face to face, who did*
> *all those miraculous signs and wonders the LORD*
> *sent him to do in Egypt—to Pharaoh and to all his*
> *officials and to his whole land. For no one has ever*
> *shown the mighty power or performed the awesome*
> *deeds that Moses did in the sight of all Israel*
> (Deuteronomy 34:10-12).

It took 80 years for the Lord to get Moses ready for the job and then 40 more years of having Moses lead the Israelites to the Promised Land. He died at 120 years old. I'd say that is a life totally given to the cause of being a trusted servant to the Most High. Surely that is worth all the space and all the time!

The Lord gave Moses great helpmates throughout his journey. They were his brother Aaron and his sister Miriam. And God also gave him one God-prepared, talented, and able assistant— Joshua. Not only was he a terrific help to Moses, but the Lord was also grooming him to take over. I am certain Joshua was excited and truly sincere in his willingness to do whatever was needed. But as an assistant, you are still not the "top dog." So the buck did not stop with him. He still lived in the safety net of his boss. Everything changed in Joshua 1:2-5 when the Lord said to Joshua:

> *"Moses my servant is dead. Now then, you and all these people, get ready to cross the Jordan River into the land I am about to give to them—to the Israelites. I will give you every place where you set your foot, as I promised Moses. Your territory will extend from the desert to Lebanon, and from the great river, the Euphrates—all the Hittite country— to the Great Sea on the west. No one will be able to stand up against you all the days of your life. As I was with Moses, so I will be with you; I will never leave you nor forsake you."* ☦

Oh boy, the time had arrived! Moses had died, and the Lord now looked to Joshua. Yes, he had just been given much power and authority, but along with that comes responsibility. As the Lord had prepared Moses for his assignment, the Lord also had prepared Joshua for this moment in time. Watch the Lord's hand at work:

1. Joshua was Moses' servant (Exodus 24:13).
2. Joshua was from the tribe of Ephraim.
3. Ephraim's descendents were the most powerful tribe in the north.

4. "Ephraim" was often used to describe the northern kingdom as a whole (Joshua 19:50).
5. Joshua was Moses' general who led the troops in the actual fighting against the Amalekites while Aaron and Hur held up Moses' hands (Exodus 17:8-13).
6. Joshua was on the mountain when Moses received the law (Exodus 32:17).
7. Joshua was one of the twelve spies Moses sent to investigate Canaan (Numbers 13:8).
8. The Lord selected Joshua to be Moses' successor long before Moses' death (Numbers 27:15-23).
9. Joshua was a military leader, a political leader, and a spiritual leader. He was not intimidated by his new responsibilities or the task that the Lord laid before him, for he knew God had been and would continue to be with him. Isn't God awesome!

So, right off the bat, God gave Joshua all that he needed—Himself. God is always enough, for any and every situation. But for a brief moment in time, Joshua took his eyes off the Lord and looked at his new job only through his own strength. I'm pretty sure that he felt overwhelmed, inadequate, and downright scared to death. But then in verses 6-9 God said:

> *"Be strong and courageous, because you will lead these people to inherit the land I swore to their forefathers to give them. Be strong and very courageous. Be careful to obey all the law my servant Moses gave you; do not turn from it to the right or to the left, that you may be successful wherever you go. Do not let this Book of the Law depart from your mouth; meditate on it day and night, so that you may be careful to do everything written in it. Then you will be prosperous and successful. Have I not commanded you? Be strong and courageous. Do not be terrified; do not be discouraged, for the LORD your God will be with you wherever you go."*

That did it! Joshua's faith was back! In fact, in the very next verse, Joshua was strong, courageous, and giving orders. God was now able to work through him, just the way God intended. What an encouraging promise to Joshua. God promised to be with him through it all—every minute. I'm sure you know what I am about to say. These Old Testament words of our Lord are still talking right to you and me today. YES, THEY ARE! These words are perfect for you and me exactly when we need them as well. Maybe right now, you need to hear the Lord say, *"As I was with Moses, so I will be with you"* (v.5a). Maybe you need to hear Him say to you right now, *"Do not be terrified; do not be discouraged, for the LORD your God will be with you wherever you go"* (v.9).

What comfort—what strength—what Truth! It reminds me of when the apostle Paul honestly expressed his desire of having a thorn in his flesh (of some type) removed. He pleaded with the Lord to take it away from him. Paul said that the Lord's answer to him was NO, but God also said to him, *"My grace is sufficient for you, for my power is made perfect in weakness"* (2 Corinthians 12:9a).

Again, I say that it is a big step in our earthly journey when we FINALLY believe that God is enough. Paul even goes on to say after his lesson learned:

> *Therefore I will boast all the more gladly about my weaknesses, so that Christ's power may rest on me. That is why, for Christ's sake, I delight in weaknesses, in insults, in hardships, in persecutions, in difficulties. For when I am weak, then I am strong* (2 Corinthians 12:9b-10).

Who in their right human mind would stand on a mountain top and boast of what they were NOT good at. In this day and age everyone is blowing their own horn of Me! Me! Me! louder and louder. Paul says that it is a great day when one knows when one CAN'T, but God CAN. God is not going to push His way in. He is patient and waits until we admit our weaknesses, and then He is more than able to take over. The results are overwhelming. I was wracking my brain trying to come up with a personal illustration for this, and I was stumped until the Lord gently hit me over the head with His special kind of two-by-four and made me see what I am doing RIGHT NOW. I can't do this to His praise, honor, and glory without Him! I don't have to think back, it's happening to me right now with every word I write. How humbling! But I do believe that is exactly where He wants us to be, humble before Him—needing Him every step of the way. And that is exactly where He told Joshua He would be with him—every step of the way.

There stood the entire nation of Israel at the Jordan River—the only thing that stood between them and the Promised Land. What a sight! But Joshua knew that he had to seek the Lord's guidance for their every move and not be hasty. He wanted to be prepared and wanted no surprises. He also knew that the first major city they would have to conquer was the city of Jericho. So he sent two spies into that city to scope it out. Those spies had to be very special, brave, trained, discreet, intelligent men who were committed to the cause—maybe like a couple of FBI men. One of our son's best friends from college is in the FBI, and what he had to go through to train for that job is mind boggling. And believe me, he is one smart cookie. I say it this way because I don't believe Joshua would be "slip-shod" and send just anybody. These two spies were hand picked, for sure.

These two spies went to the house of a prostitute named Rahab and stayed there. Naughty men? Absolutely not! It was a good place to gather information and have no questions asked of them in return. Rahab's house was in an ideal location for a quick escape because it was built into the city wall. But the REAL reason the spies stayed there was because God had (unknown to her) an "appointment" with Rahab. He had plans for her. He was ready to deal with her heart and give her new potential to serve Him. God used these spies to get the ball rolling. The king of Jericho was told about these spies. Rahab had hidden the men on her roof top; and when the king's men came to her house looking for them, she told them the spies had already left, but if they hurried, they could catch them. Yes, that was a lie. Does God approve of lying? No, of course He doesn't. But she was doing what she did best. This kind of deception was just a part of her life. Actually, she hadn't even confessed her faith in God yet.

There are two theological words which help explain what our spiritual journey is: Justified and Sanctified. When we accept Christ as our Savior, justification happens in a split second. When people tell me they can't remember the exact day and time they did that, I first tell them to just think back to when Jesus became real to them, when their lives started to change: there was a second in time when their whole eternal destination was changed. The Bible also says that when a sinner repents, the angels rejoice. So that pretty much tells me there WAS an exact time. That word is called JUSTIFIED. We have been justified—made right in the eyes of God—because now He sees us through the blood of His Son. So then, what He sees when He looks at us, is someone who is right, pure, and blameless. Isn't that the best? You and I are still sinners, and yet we can go boldly into God's presence (and He can't look at sin–Habakkuk 1:13a), because His Son has made us right. I stand in awe of that as I write this. Hearing that over and over NEVER gets boring to me.

Our salvation happens in a second, but our transformation into the likeness of Christ continues throughout the rest of our earthly lives. That word is called SANCTIFICATION. Every Christian is in the process of being sanctified, and not a one of us is there yet. Philippians 1:6, *being confident of this, that he who began a good work in you will carry it on to completion until the day of Christ Jesus.*

That's why our Christian walk with the Lord is a step-by-step process. Rahab was going to start her spiritual journey with the Lord. He was beginning a good work in her on her salvation day, just like He did for you and me. *By faith the prostitute Rahab, because she welcomed the spies, was not killed with those who were disobedient* (Hebrews 11:31).

I love the way Rahab went to the roof top to ask the spies some questions. She had good street sense from running her "business," and that meant listening. She had heard how the Lord had dried up the Red Sea, and how the Israelites had defeated two kings and their kingdoms east of the Jordan. The news was out! Israel's God is real! She confessed that the Lord WAS the God of heaven and earth. That was her personal confession. And THAT, my friend, is what our God is waiting to hear from every one of us at some moment in time. Then she requested kindness for herself and her family. This time she added, *"Now then, please swear to me by the LORD...."* Already she knew where to look for truth. Yes, she was a prostitute; but the Lord was now working on her heart. Who knows, maybe she never even wanted to be a prostitute, but to support her family she may have had to do whatever it took. I don't know that, but she did love her family and certainly included them immediately in her request. The spies agreed, and gave her specific instructions to follow in Joshua 2:17-21:

> *The men said to her, "This oath you made us swear will not be binding on us unless, when we enter the land, you have tied this scarlet cord in the window through which you let us down, and unless you have brought your father and mother, your brothers and all your family into your house. If anyone goes outside your house into the street, his blood will be on his own head; we will not be responsible. As for anyone who is in the house with you, his blood will be on our head if a hand is laid on him. But if you tell what we are doing, we will be released from the oath you made us swear."*
>
> *"Agreed," she replied. "Let it be as you say." So she sent them away and they departed. And she tied the scarlet cord in the window.*

She agreed to the terms and also told the spies to go to the hills so their pursuers would not find them. She told them to hide there for three days, until their pursuers had returned to town, so they could safely be on their way. Now wouldn't you think that by this time the spies were very anxious to get back to Joshua and report their findings? Well, nevertheless, they did exactly what Rahab told them. That speaks loudly about Rahab, if you ask me. In 2:24, the spies gave this report when they got back to Joshua, *"The LORD has surely given the whole land into our hands; all the people are melting in fear because of us"* (v.24b).

That was exactly the report Joshua wanted to hear.

Joshua now started the detailed planning. First they needed to cross the Jordan River, but it was at flood stage (all a part of God's plan). The Lord wanted to remind Joshua what He had done for Moses and show Joshua he could count on the same power of God to be on his side to overcome the impossible. Joshua was an eyewitness to the Lord parting the Red Sea during the Exodus from Egypt. So he knew what the Lord was able to do. God held the flow of the river back so that all could cross.

> *Now the Jordan is at flood stage all during harvest. Yet as soon as the priests who carried the ark reached the Jordan and their feet touched the water's edge, the water from upstream stopped flowing. It piled up in a heap a great distance away, at a town called Adam in the vicinity of Zarethan, while the water flowing down to the Sea of the Arabah (the Salt Sea) was completely cut off. So the people crossed over opposite Jericho. The priests who carried the ark of the covenant of the LORD stood firm on dry ground in the middle of the Jordan, while all Israel passed by until the whole nation had completed the crossing on dry ground (Joshua 3:15-17).*

Joshua was a military man. I expect he was ready to conquer Jericho by force. He probably was shining up his sword and getting the military in order. How else would you take down a city of this magnitude? But the Lord had other plans, and to make sure they were carried out, this is what happened to Joshua.

> *Now when Joshua was near Jericho, he looked up and saw a man standing in front of him with a drawn sword in his hand. Joshua went up to him and asked, "Are you for us or for our enemies?"*
>
> *"Neither," he replied, "but as commander of the army of the LORD I have now come." Then Joshua fell facedown to the ground in reverence,*

and asked him, "What message does my Lord have
for his servant?"
        The commander of the LORD's army replied,
"Take off your sandals, for the place where you are
standing is holy." And Joshua did so (5:13-15).

I don't know if Joshua was falling into the human trap of self confidence or not, but there was a reason why he had to have a "holy ground" experience, just like his predecessor Moses had. Before Moses started for Egypt, and before Joshua began the takeover of the land of Canaan, both needed to know just WHO was in charge and WHO always is the better One to be in charge. Both needed to know just Who's instructions, no matter how seemingly unreasonable, were to be obeyed. We all need to take our sandals off more often and realize the ground we stand on is holy, because He is with us, and He is in charge. We would be so much better off, and prevent so much trouble, if we would just keep those "sandals" off. It's all about knowing the sovereignty of God. He is God and we are not. He wants us humble before Him, and that is simply keeping Him in His place as we stay in ours.

The Lord gave Joshua the instructions regarding how they were going to take down Jericho. If Joshua hadn't just had that experience crossing the Jordan with God, I think there might have been some questions. This experienced military man was told to take down a city and NOT use any weapons. What? We're just going to walk around the walls, and play some trumpets and then give a loud shout? Are you serious? In chapter 6, Joshua gave the order to "Advance!"—no questioning, no debate, no disagreements in policy. In fact, in 6:2, the Lord told Joshua before they even began the mission that He had already delivered Jericho into their hands, along with its king and fighting men. Victory before you even face your foe. Not a bad way to face the enemy!

Do you realize that is exactly how you and I face our enemy? Every day we face the enemy of our soul (Satan and his followers). Every day we face trials, or another way to put it is, we face our "vast armies." We think that they are impossible to overcome. We feel we'll never survive. We feel like giving up. Well, take heart! The battle has already been won. It was won for you and me on the

Cross. Just like the Israelites when they had to face the battle of Jericho. They had to step out and trust that God's Words were true; we have to do the same. As long as we live on this earth, we will face the vast armies who desire our destruction; and we, too, have to step out and trust that God's Words are true.

In Revelation, the apostle John tells us that Satan will be banished into eternal hell, and so will evil of every kind. Then we, His precious children, will be a part of a new heaven and a new earth where we will live in perfection again with our God, just the way He intended it to be when He created us. That's how God's story goes for His children. WE WIN! Somehow it is a whole lot easier facing our world today when we already know the ending, wouldn't you say?

God's instructions were to destroy everything and everyone. Yes, there is a lot of killing in the Old Testament. But it gives us a glimpse of God's judgment. The people of Jericho, the Bible says, all heard the stories, just like Rahab. They had a choice and a chance, just like Rahab. Same principle, different story. God's simple command of obedience reaps blessings; disobedience reaps consequences. All the silver and gold and the articles of bronze and iron were to go into the Lord's treasury. Simple instructions. Not rocket science. And just as the Lord said it would happen, the walls of Jericho came tumbling down, and everyone was destroyed except for Rahab and her family. She and her family were engrafted into the family of the Israelites. She married and became a mom. This woman had quite the past, but because she chose to believe in the One and only God, she found herself loved unconditionally, forgiven, and she became the mother of a son named Boaz. (Keep that fact in the back of your mind as we will see Boaz again in our study.)

What a great victory! Word of this victory spread throughout the land, and yet I have to say, but.... Whenever one is dealing with human beings, even in the best of stories, there is usually a "but." One man, named Achan, disobeyed. The temptation was just too great for him. You know, that's not really true. According to I Corinthians 10:13, no temptation is too great IF we go to the Lord for help.

No temptation has seized you except what is
common to man. And God is faithful; he will not let
you be tempted beyond what you can bear. But when
you are tempted, he will also provide a way out so
that you can stand up under it.

Temptation can be bigger than you and me, but it is not
bigger than the Holy Spirit of God if we choose to tap into His
power. Temptation doesn't just happen. It is a series of events that,
at any time we choose, can be stopped and will never materialize into
an action. It's like that silly little saying, which is so true. When it
comes to temptation, "You can't help it if a bird flies over your head,
but you can help whether it makes a nest in your hair." Living in this
world, we are going to be tempted. There is no getting away from it.
But, the choice comes down to what we do with the temptation.
With the Holy Spirit's power, we can just say no by taking that
thought and making it captive to the Lord Jesus, Himself.
Temptation gone! When you start playing with the temptation, it
will pull you in and hold you like a wild animal's claws hold on to its
prey.
　　　Achan started playing around with his temptation. In his
series of events, he admitted that he first looked and saw the
plunder—there was a beautiful robe, silver, and gold—and he started
thinking too much. He started thinking how good he would look in
that robe, and how all the silver and gold could help his family, and
then the Bible says he coveted. He still had time to run, but he took
it and hid it in the ground inside his tent. Now if he didn't think it
was wrong, why did he go to such great lengths to hide it? He lived
in the illusion that no one saw what he was doing. But the Lord did.
Through the next battle with the enemy (Joshua 7), the Lord made it
clear to Joshua that something was dreadfully wrong. Joshua had
sent about three thousand men to go up against the enemy, Ai.
Thirty-six of them were killed and the rest chased from the city gate
and then were struck down. Joshua was devastated. When he went
to the Lord and fell face down, the Lord made it clear to him what
had happened and why. The Lord instructed Joshua to have the
people present themselves for a tribe-by-tribe, clan-by-clan search,
and Achan was found out. Achan and his entire family, his livestock,

and even his tent were destroyed. Over Achan they heaped up a large pile of rocks, which remains to this day. God made them set up this reminder so that every time they see that pile of rocks, they remember that God commands obedience. That's all there is to it!

God used Joshua in a mighty way to destroy the enemies and gain the Land of Milk and Honey—the Promised Land. God helped him defeat thirty-one kings and nations in all. But as time went by, Joshua grew old. He knew that his calling was about finished. But he had one final farewell speech. Again, I tried to shorten it, but it is just too good. Listen to his powerful words in Joshua 23:2b-16:

"I am old and well advanced in years. 3You yourselves have seen everything the LORD your God has done to all these nations for your sake; it was the LORD your God who fought for you. 4Remember how I have allotted as an inheritance for your tribes all the land of the nations that remain—the nations I conquered—between the Jordan and the Great Sea in the west. 5The LORD your God himself will drive them out of your way. He will push them out before you, and you will take possession of their land, as the LORD your God promised you.

6"Be very strong; be careful to obey all that is written in the Book of the Law of Moses, without turning aside to the right or to the left. 7Do not associate with these nations that remain among you; do not invoke the names of their gods or swear by them. You must not serve them or bow down to them. 8But you are to hold fast to the LORD your God, as you have until now.

9"The LORD has driven out before you great and powerful nations; to this day no one has been able to withstand you. 10One of you routs a thousand, because the LORD your God fights for you, just as he promised. 11So be very careful to love the LORD your God.

12"But if you turn away and ally yourselves with the survivors of these nations that remain among you and if you intermarry with them and associate with them, 13then you may be sure that the LORD your God will no longer drive out these nations before you. Instead, they will become snares and traps for you, whips on your backs and thorns in your eyes, until you perish from this good land, which the LORD your God has given you.

14"Now I am about to go the way of all the earth. You know with all your heart and soul that not one of all the good promises the LORD your God gave you has failed. Every promise has been fulfilled; not one has failed. 15But just as every good promise of the LORD your God has come true, so the LORD will bring on you all the evil he has threatened, until he has destroyed you from this good land he has given you. 16If you violate the covenant of the LORD your God, which he commanded you, and go and serve other gods and bow down to them, the LORD's anger will burn against you, and you will quickly perish from the good land he has given you."

I was especially touched by verse six. Joshua directed the very same thought to them as God had said to him in chapter one when Joshua had stood at the beginning of the unknown. He knew these words were true and were the best advice and gift he could leave the chosen people of God. Joshua gave the people a choice because God does not force Himself on anyone. He came right out and said that if you feel it's undesirable for you to serve the Lord, that's your call, *"...But as for me and my household, we will serve the LORD"* (Joshua 24:15b). Is your choice evident to those around you? If we are sure of something, it is very easy to pass it on. Because if you are really sold on your product—if you really know that your product works, it's so easy to sell. If you and I are absolutely convinced of this gospel message, we WILL be sharing it. And, in turn, we will be selling it through our words, yes, but also through our changed lives. Because please remember, God is watching—He never sleeps! (Psalm 121:3-4.)

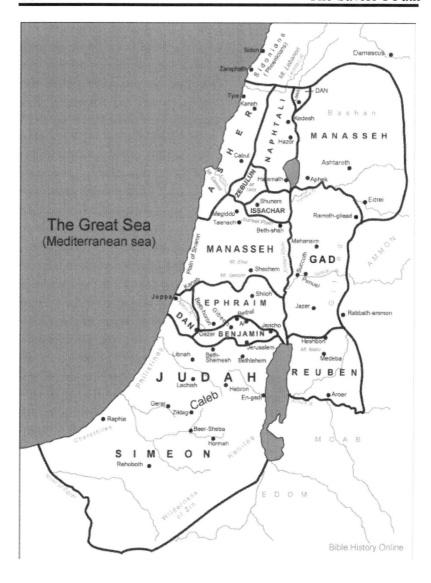

CHAPTER 7

JESUS'   SIGNPOSTS

"Obey the Law": ✝ Pg. 150

Despite Moses' plea to obey carefully all the words of the law, the Israelites failed; just as all did thereafter, which continues on into our day—except Jesus.

● ...Matthew 5:17, *"Do not think that I have come to abolish the Law or the Prophets; I have not come to abolish them but to fulfill them.*

"Forsake You": ✝ Pg. 151

On the cross, in some mysterious, unexplainable way, Jesus as the perfect Son of God and Son of Man, took upon Himself all of mankind's past, present, and future sin. And at that moment, God the Father turned away from His precious Son as punishment for my sin and yours. He forsook His Son at that judgment moment so He will not have to forsake us who call on Jesus as our Lord and Savior. Praise be to God! Thank you, Jesus!

● ...Matthew 27:46, *About the ninth hour Jesus cried out in a loud voice, "Eloi, Eloi, lama sabachthani?"--which means, "My God, my God, why have you forsaken me?"*

Lesson 7: Joshua

1.   In Deuteronomy 32:44-47, what were Moses' last instructions to the Israelites? How much did he mean it, and how sure was he that it was the truth? (vs. 47.)

2.   How did Moses die, and Who buried him? (Deut. 34.)

3.   Joshua 1. Who took over for Moses in leading the people into the Promised Land?

4.   What do you think Joshua was pondering right about the time he took over? What did the Lord promise him? What were the Lord's clear instructions to him?

5.   What does the apostle Paul say to do in II Corinthians 12:9 when you feel inadequate?

6.   Where did Joshua send the two spies? Why did he send them out? Where did they stay? (Joshua 2.)

7.   How much faith does the Lord require to start your adventure with Him? (Luke 17:6.) How did Rahab demonstrate God's forgiveness and love? (Matthew 1:5.)

8.   What did the spies promise Rahab?

9.   Explain what happened to Joshua in his "burning bush" experience in Joshua 5:13-15. Any idea why he needed one, too? Why does everyone need an experience like that one at one time or another?

10. How was Jericho captured? What was the "military strategy"? Who should always get the credit, even though He borrows humans' bodies to do the job?

11. In the Old Testament, you see so much destruction and killing. But, if Rahab surrendered her life to the Lord and believed Him with all her heart, did everyone in Jericho also have a choice? Does everyone have a choice? (Romans 1:20.) According to God's Word, what will happen to everyone who disobeys and rebels against the Holy Spirit, God the Father, and His Son? (Revelation 20:11-15.) What is the unpardonable sin? (Luke 12:10.)

12. What were Joshua's final words of instruction to the Israelites in Joshua 23? What was his choice and final proclamation? What does that mean when you choose to post those words in your home?

8

The Judges

The Promised Land was being conquered one nation at a time. The Lord had used Joshua, the military warrior, in a mighty way. Before Joshua died, he divided the land among the twelve tribes of Israel. We know from Scripture as we begin the study of the Judges that during the lifetime of Joshua the people of Israel served the Lord. But in Judges 2:10-15, the tables turned:

> *After that whole generation had been gathered to their fathers, another generation grew up, who knew neither the LORD nor what he had done for Israel. Then the Israelites did evil in the eyes of the LORD and served the Baals. They forsook the LORD, the God of their fathers, who had brought them out of Egypt. They followed and worshiped various gods of the peoples around them. They provoked the LORD to anger because they forsook him and served Baal and the Ashtoreths. In his anger against Israel the LORD handed them over to raiders who plundered them. He sold them to their enemies all around, whom they were no longer able to resist. Whenever Israel went out to fight, the hand of the LORD was against them to defeat them, just as he had sworn to them. They were in great distress.*

That is an understatement. They were a mess! We should not be surprised, and they shouldn't have been either, because the simple command is constant: Obey the Lord and He will bless; disobey and He will see to it that you know what you have done!

This leads to an issue on the love of God. As human beings, we have a tendency to want to believe that because God loves us, He will see to it that nothing bad happens to us. Oh, there is no doubt in my mind that God wants the best for us, but sometimes the best for us means disaster. There are times throughout Scripture that the writer will say, *Wake up!* (Revelation 3:2.) That means, open your eyes and see what you are doing! Take a look at the path you are going down and see where it is leading! WAKE UP! God knows us so well, and loves us so much, that there are times when He, in His sovereignty, makes us wake up. He gives us a good shake up. And how does He do that? Let me tell you, it doesn't look good. Yes, it IS good, but at the time, it doesn't always look good. Paul writes in Romans 8: 28-29a:

> *And we know that in all things God works for the good of those who love him, who have been called according to his purpose. For those God foreknew he also predestined to be conformed to the likeness of his Son.*

Paul understood that God has to do what He has to do to fulfill His purpose in all of us, and that is to turn us into the very likeness of Christ. To be like Jesus. Now, that's a project! That is going to take work! Turning you and me into the likeness of Jesus. That sounds wonderful! Well then, expect some wake up calls.

When our first grandchild, Jenna, was a small girl, we bought her a little bike to ride when she was at our house. I remember the first day she rode it. She looked adorable on it. I was out there watching, making sure she stayed in the driveway. I told her she could NOT go on the road. She looked at me like she understood completely and then rode right onto the road. The way she looked at me when she did it, I knew that the problem was not a lack of understanding. So I sternly told her again not to go on the road, and if she did, I would take her bike away because I loved her too much to let her get hurt. She turned her bike around and rode right back onto the road. I didn't say a word. I just took her off the bike and put the bike back into the garage. Oh, if looks could kill! And then she said, "You are a mean grandma." Can you imagine how that broke my heart? I wanted to give that bike back to her, because she has other grandmas, and I didn't want to be known as the MEAN one. But I knew I couldn't. She had to learn. And it's true— I do love her too much to see her get hurt, so I had to do it.

That is exactly how the Lord has to treat HIS stubborn, strong-willed children. I'm sure that He "hears" us call Him mean, too, when He has to discipline us. Yes, discipline IS painful, but it teaches us, and that is the goal. We are a people that have to be taught how to do life right. Jesus said that He wanted us to have a life that was abundant—full to the brim of the best He has to offer. So if that takes some disciplining, so be it. He loves us too much to let us stay in the place we're at. I don't think it changes His mind even a little bit when He sees us shake our little fists and call Him mean, for He knows that it's going to turn out for our good. God has a whole different definition of good than we do, doesn't He? But that's good!

Israel needed a wake up call, for sure. I am amazed at the line in Scripture where it clearly states that the very next generation didn't know the Lord (Judges 2:10). The very next generation? How could that be? I'll tell you. NO ONE TOLD THEM! ✞ Again, I am reminded of what Paul said to the people of Rome. He made it so clear in Romans 10:14:

> *How, then, can they call on the one they have not*
> *believed in? And how can they believe in the one of*
> *whom they have not heard? And how can they hear*
> *without someone preaching to them?*

What concerns me is why they didn't tell their children. If you have the greatest news in the whole world, it is next to impossible to keep that to yourself, right? The first thing you want to do when you get some good news is to share it. If something is of utmost importance to you, if it has changed your life, and if nothing else can explain the reason why you are the way you are, or have what you have, or experienced what you have experienced, then you tell everyone all about it, and probably not just once, but over and over again. Makes you think, doesn't it? Am I so convinced of what Jesus has done for me that I can't help but share it? Or if I am NOT convinced, maybe I am ashamed of the gospel of Jesus Christ. Are you sharing Jesus with your next generation? Why or why not? Only you can answer that question.

I know of one person who was convinced of the gospel of Christ and was not ashamed—Fanny Crosby. Because of a doctor's mistake, at six weeks old she became blind. As she grew up, she had a grandma who taught her God's Word, and she memorized chapter after chapter. When she grew older and understood what had happened to her and why, because of the Word in her heart, she did not sin by choosing bitterness and self-pity, but rather she chose to accept the fact that the Lord knew what had to be done for her to accomplish His purpose in her life. And what was that, you ask? God's purpose for her was to know Him so well that out of the overflow of her heart she wrote poem after poem that became song after song. God wanted you and me singing, "Blessed Assurance, Jesus is Mine." The best part of the abundant life is KNOWING without a doubt that we have a Savior, that we have HOPE, and that we have a FUTURE. That is a great way to live even when life is filled with obstacles. When life feels hopeless, it is not because of your circumstances, but because you don't know your Savior. That, my friend, can change. You DO have a choice. You do not have to live in hopelessness. If you've had your wake up call, and you want so much to sing that you have the security of the blessed assurance of your Savior and of your future Home, here's the way: All you have to do is believe in your heart and confess with your mouth that you know you are a sinner, that you have been offered a Savior, and then accept that precious Gift. The Bible says that if you do that, you will be saved—from yourself, from your sins, from God's wrath, and from hell. That's quite a salvation gift, wouldn't you say? And it's yours for the asking! Hey, how about right now? Today is the day of salvation! Your day!

Because of the awful state of Israel's faith in God, He could have said that enough was enough; but again, He was determined to get the Savior to this world, so He raised up judges ☩ who saved them out of their enemies' hands. All the judges seemed to have some defect or handicap—not as a hindrance, but with a positive outcome—under the direction of a Sovereign God. In other words, God used and still uses ordinary people (even those with a defect) to accomplish His great purposes. For example, some ordinary people included those having no skills, those getting the job by marrying into it, those being left-handed, or a woman, etc. I think you get what I am saying. God always seems to use unqualified people to prove they can be effective through Him. So really, we all are ordinary people with our own defects. But some people don't THINK that they are, and they miss out; because sometimes they aren't chosen for God's service because THEY THINK they are so strong, or THEY THINK they are so capable. Read what Paul says in I Corinthians 1:27-29:

> *But God chose the foolish things of the world to shame the wise; God chose the weak things of the world to shame the strong. He chose the lowly things of this world and the despised things—and the things that are not—to nullify the things that are, so that no one may boast before him.*

Some of the judges were more willing to surrender to the Lord's leading than others. Some of them did great things, and the Lord gave them success; others chose to be more concerned about themselves, and not much was done during their time in office. It's very clear in the book of the Judges that God used ordinary and flawed people for His service, sometimes even when they were unwilling to surrender to His will, His guidance, and His Holy Spirit; but they didn't receive God's blessings due to their unwillingness to obey. There is no room for smart-alecks in the Lord's service.

Here is a list of the judges of Israel that we are going to look at in our study:

Othneil
Ehud
Shamgar
Deborah
Gideon
Abimelech
Tola
Jair

Jephthah
Ibzan
Elon
Abdon
Samson
Eli
Samuel

I am going to mention a few in detail because their examples have important lessons to teach us. Let's start with Deborah. Why was a woman picked? She was married. There was a man in charge of the armed forces. I dare say she was chosen because she was the only one who dared to accept God's call, understanding that she couldn't do it, but that HE could do it through her. She was a willing vessel to be used. It is interesting to note that she was the only judge said to have been a prophetess. There are not many out there, you know, otherwise Jesus would not have said, *"The harvest is plentiful, but the workers are few"* (Luke 10:2a). Deborah was a willing worker, and the Lord used her in a brave and great way.

Gideon was just minding his own business, threshing wheat, when the angel of the Lord came to him and said, *"The LORD is with you, mighty warrior"* (Judges 6:12b). I dare say that Gideon was never called that before. He might have even looked around to see if the angel was talking to someone else. Yes, the Lord sometimes calls those who least expect it. So it shouldn't surprise us that Gideon asked for fleeces, just to make sure he was hearing right. He felt insignificant, insufficient, and inadequate. Yeah! That's exactly the way the Lord wants you to feel. Then you are far more apt to depend on Him and follow His leading. God made it VERY clear that Gideon was the man of His choice, and God used him, too, in a mighty way. Unfortunately, it went to Gideon's head, and even though he had done such good things for the Lord, his example shows us that we will always have to fight against the repercussions of "self importance."

J. Vernon McGee, one of my favorite old-time preachers, once told a true story to prove how useless we are without the proper power. He said he was at the Rose Bowl Parade in Pasadena, California, the year that the United States entered World War II.

Standard Oil had the most magnificent float in the parade. It had a patriotic theme from front to back. The theme was, "Be Prepared." He went on to say that the most unbelievable thing happened right before his eyes. In the middle of the parade route, the float ran out of gas! Standard Oil of all companies! Come on! How embarrassing! McGee went on to explain that is exactly what Christians do. We try to live a Christian life. When we try to be like Christ on our own power, we run out of gas fast! As critical as one might be of Standard Oil, we, too, should be embarrassed to try to live for Christ without the Power. We Christians, of all people, should be overflowing with power because the Power Source is endless. We need a cause. A cause gets you up in the morning with purpose, and there is no greater cause than, under the power of the Holy Spirit, living your life for the One who created you, saved you, and called you by name to serve Him. We do NOT have an excuse for running low on or running out of gas.

Then there is Samson. There is much written about his story, but God wants us to learn a big lesson through this guy. How sad that so many of our Bible stories in Sunday School have elevated him just because he was so strong. When I heard this story as a young child, the story was all about Samson. That's the trouble, and we are going to see that there is NO man worthy of elevation for doing good, because the proper credit belongs to God.

Before Samson was born, an angel of the Lord came to a childless couple to tell them that they were going to have a son. He would be a Nazirite (a member of a class of people especially devoted to God). The angel of the Lord went on to explain:

> *"because you will conceive and give birth to a son.*
> *No razor may be used on his head, because the boy*
> *is to be a Nazirite, set apart to God from birth, and*
> *he will begin the deliverance of Israel from the*
> *hands of the Philistines"* (Judges 13:5).

After Samson was born, the Lord blessed him as he grew. And the Spirit of the Lord began to stir him. He was on the right track. He was heading in the right direction. As an only child, and after they had waited so long and heard those promises about their son, I have a feeling his parents spoiled him. It's so easy to give our children what they want all the time thinking that it is what will make them happy, or maybe we try to give them what we never had. You've heard the phrase—spoiled rotten. That is what happened here. Samson became demanding. He demanded a Philistine wife, and that was forbidden. As head of the family, the father exercised authority in all matters, often including the choice of wives for his sons (Genesis 24:3-9, Nehemiah 10:30). But if that was what Samson wanted, that was what Samson got, even though they tried their best to persuade him otherwise.

> *(His parents did not know that this was from the LORD, who was seeking an occasion to confront the Philistines; for at that time they were ruling over Israel.)* (Judges 14:4.)

God had given Samson unusual strength. That strength was given to him by God, for God's purposes, although Samson misused this gift continuously. For many of us, when Delilah came into the story, we blamed her for her deception and Samson's downfall. We are led to believe that Samson's strength came from his hair. I think he believed it, too. So when Delilah finally wore him down, and Samson said his strength was in his hair, and that it was not to be cut, we cry out, "NO Samson, don't tell her!" When his hair was cut, and his strength was gone, we were devastated. It wasn't a haircut that removed his strength, GOD DID! He had had it! Samson was a disappointment. He failed to do the job God predestined for him. Yes, God knew this would happen all the time, so why did He even tell his parents what he told them? It's because He is teaching. God is always teaching and showing us our frail humanity. Special note here: The Lord uses even the sinful weaknesses of men to accommodate His purposes and bring praise to His name (Genesis 45:8, 50:20, 2 Chronicles 25:20, Acts 2:23, 4:28, Romans 8:28-29). In Judges 13:5, the angel of God did say that he will BEGIN the deliverance, not take it to completion.

After Samson was captured by the Philistines, from Judges 16:21-22:

Then the Philistines seized him, gouged out his eyes and took him down to Gaza. Binding him with bronze shackles, they set him to grinding in the prison. But the hair on his head began to grow again after it had been shaved.

When the Philistines, one of the enemies of Israel, wanted some entertainment, they shouted to bring Samson out. I'm sure as a huge joke, they could laugh at this poor blind sap, who once had unbelievable power but now could only flounder and flop around. Yea, what a laugh! Samson prayed in Judges 16:28b. My first thought when I read that he prayed, was, "Great!" He finally came to his senses and realized how he had failed God's purpose, and he wanted to end his life making amends. At least at the end of his life he could fulfill something for his Sovereign God because that's how he started his prayer. However, just listen to why he wanted his strength back. *"O Sovereign LORD, remember me. O God, please strengthen me just once more, and let me with one blow get revenge on the Philistines for my two eyes."*

So it wasn't for the Lord, it was the same old Samson. It's all about him. It's always been all about him. What good came from this sad story, and why is he listed in Hebrews 11? The only thing I can see is that in the end he recognized that his strength came from God, and because in his dying act he demonstrated that faith. Just a thought, when the Lord gives us an extraordinary gift, how tempting it is to take the credit—to be proud of our accomplishments. But when He gives us a gift, it is never for our personal gain; it has been given to us for His gain in this world. Let's look at the verses where God did utilize His purpose for Samson.

From Judges 15:3-5 and 14-15 we read these verses:

Samson said to them, "This time I have a right to get even with the Philistines; I will really harm them." So he went out and caught three hundred foxes and tied them tail to tail in pairs. He then fastened a torch to every pair of tails, lit the torches and let the foxes loose in the standing grain of the Philistines. He burned up the shocks and standing grain, together with the vineyards and olive groves.

As he approached Lehi, the Philistines came toward him shouting. The Spirit of the LORD came upon him in power. The ropes on his arms became like charred flax, and the bindings dropped from his hands. Finding a fresh jawbone of a donkey, he grabbed it and struck down a thousand men.

And from Judges 16: 25-30:

While they were in high spirits, they shouted, "Bring out Samson to entertain us." So they called Samson out of the prison, and he performed for them.
When they stood him among the pillars, Samson said to the servant who held his hand, "Put me where I can feel the pillars that support the temple, so that I may lean against them." Now the temple was crowded with men and women; all the rulers of the Philistines were there, and on the roof were about three thousand men and women watching Samson perform. Then Samson prayed to the LORD, "O Sovereign LORD, remember me. O God, please strengthen me just once more, and let me with one blow get revenge on the Philistines for my two eyes." Then Samson reached toward the two central pillars on which the temple stood. Bracing himself against them, his right hand on the one and his left hand on the other, Samson said, "Let me die with the Philistines!" Then he pushed with all his might, and down came the temple on the rulers and all the people in it. Thus he killed many more when he died than while he lived.

Israel was ruled by judges for over 300 years. Eli and Samuel were the last of those judges. Eli wasn't one of the strongest judges, either. He tended to react to situations rather than to take decisive action. God wants us to be sure of His leading and then act on it! He wants us confident, knowing that He would never lead us in the wrong direction. Samuel was born near the end of Eli's life, and God had big plans for Samuel because Israel had wandered away from God again. Samuel's mother, Hannah, had been childless, and she had carried that burden for a long time. One day she went to the temple to pray, and it was then that she met Eli. She was praying with such intensity that Eli thought she was drunk. High intensity prayer. It's powerful. It's not like she'd never prayed before, it's just that this time she was ready to surrender to the God who knows best the fact that she wanted a child so much. She told the Lord that if He chose to give her a son, she would give him to the Lord for all the days of his life. But when she was through praying, the Bible says that her face was no longer downcast. She was able to eat. That is someone who has peace. At that point in time, she had no idea she was going to have Samuel. So for her, the situation didn't change, but she did because she was willing to let God have His way.

The Lord blessed Hannah with a son, and she was good on her word. When the boy was weaned, she took him to the temple and presented him to the Lord, whom he would serve all the days of his life. In I Samuel 2:26, it says, *And the boy Samuel continued to grow in stature and in favor with the LORD and with men.* And chapter 7:15 says, *Samuel continued as judge over Israel all the days of his life.*

When Samuel was old, he appointed his sons as judges for Israel, but his sons did not walk in his ways. They were dishonest, accepted bribes, and perverted justice. Not your model sons. Eli's sons were wicked, too. Both men, Eli and Samuel, were men of God in full-time ministry but they had wayward children. Maybe they were bad parents. Maybe they spent so much time in their ministry that they forgot to raise the children God had given them. We are so quick to judge and assume that is what happened. The Bible does not say why the sons went wayward, but that they just did. Now, maybe it's true. Maybe the parents didn't give their boys the time they needed, or didn't teach them what they may have assumed they already knew because of who their parents were. We just expect our children to follow our ways. Well, that's a good reason to take a look at your life and see if it IS going in the direction you would want your children to go, because children do, for the most part, seem to follow their parents' influence.

Now, having said that, there is another way to look at it. Maybe Eli and Samuel tried to be good parents, but their kids were simply bad eggs. They chose to be rebellious. They chose to follow the ways of the world. They were determined NOT to be like their spiritual nut dads.

The reason why I know there could be two sides is because we have two sons. Both were raised in the same environment with the same rules and teachings. One of our sons accepted the Lord as his Savior in his teens and just didn't fall into a rebellious nature. On the other hand, our other son chose to follow his own way, and what a way it was. We are so grateful that he didn't fall into some addiction or jail; but he was one miserable kid, which then made his parents miserable, too. In parenting, there is nothing more difficult then watching your child make decisions you know are going to cause trouble and hurt. He got into a real dark side. You wonder what you did wrong. Could you have done something different? Why didn't I see this coming? The only way I could keep from slipping into a real funk about the whole thing as it persisted for months into years, was to pray. Every morning when he left for school, and then later for work, I would go into his room and pray for just this wayward son of mine for ten minutes. Every day I surrendered him back to the Lord, knowing that only He could change our son's heart. Surrender is hard for a mom because we feel our job is to kiss our children's hurts away. We were able to do that when they were little, and it worked. Moms were able to fix anything. But this broken boy was beyond this mom's ability. I remember saying to the Lord to do whatever it takes to get his attention. I would be there to love him and pick up the broken pieces.

Our son came to know his Savior when he and his wife-to-be were at their pre-marital counseling. I had pre-warned our pastor that when he asked our son the spiritual questions, not to believe him because he didn't believe a word of what he would answer; he just knew the right answers because that's what he was taught. I knew he would think he was pretty tricky, but I was one step ahead of him. We think we can fool people by our churchy yet hypocritical answers, but we are not fooling the One who really counts. Our pastor confronted him face to face, and told him that just because his parents were in the ministry, that did not give him a free ticket to salvation. That hit him square between the eyes. He told me later that all the things I had been trying to tell him for years started to flood his heart and mind. So, discouraged parents, keep praying for your children, keep loving them, keep living out your faith, and keep talking, because they are hearing more than you think.

Now, I have a happy ending to my son's story. I am so, so grateful. Words can't express the thrill that I KNOW both of my boys are going to "be there" for all eternity. They are both in the ministry today—two extremely different ministries, because they are two different men. They look different, dress different, and act different; but if you turned them both inside out, they would look identical, because their hearts have been washed in the same blood of their Savior.

So, personally speaking, I am asking you to be cautious before you pass judgment on situations like Eli and Samuel's. We aren't told, and we just don't know. In my opinion, it could go either way. But the best thing we can do for our children is to love Jesus with all of our hearts so that His reflection is seen in us, and then our parenting will be the kind of parenting God expects when He calls us into that all-important job. But then when they are grown, we have to surrender them to the Lord, because now they make their own decisions and their own choices. As parents, we never stop falling on our knees on their behalf, no matter how old they get (even though you may need help to get up!)

As we leave this chapter of the judges, we will take Samuel with us, as the nation of Israel soon begs for a king.

CHAPTER 8

JESUS' SIGNPOSTS

"No One Told Them": ✞ Pg. 173

●...Matthew 28:18-20, *Then Jesus came to them and said, "All authority in heaven and on earth has been given to me. Therefore go and make disciples of all nations, baptizing them in the name of the Father and of the Son and of the Holy Spirit, and teaching them to obey everything I have commanded you. And surely I am with you always, to the very end of the age."*

"Raised Up Judges": ✞ Pg. 174

God has raised up Jesus <u>from the dead</u>, not only to save His people, but also to be the one and only righteous <u>Judge</u>.

●...2 Timothy 4:1a, *In the presence of God and of Christ Jesus, who will judge the living and the dead,*

●...Romans 14:10-12, *You, then, why do you judge your brother? Or why do you look down on your brother? For we will all stand before God's judgment seat. It is written: " `As surely as I live,' says the Lord, `every knee will bow before me; every tongue will confess to God.' " So then, each of us will give an account of himself to God.*

Lesson 8: The Judges
Judges and I Samuel 1-3

1.   What did the Israelites choose to do after Joshua died? (Judges 2:10-12.)

2.   Why didn't the next generation know the Lord and what He had done for Israel? What would keep one generation from telling the next? Is this a major question for today also?

3.   How are people tomorrow going to know Jesus is their Savior? (Romans 10:14-15.)

4.   When God's anger is provoked, what can you count on?

5.   From Judges 2:13-15, what did God do to Israel? Does that sound like a loving God? Is it a loving God who will do what it takes to bring His children back from sin?

6.   Why were the judges raised up? Is there something noticeable about every judge? What does that tell you? Does God want you to feel insignificant, insufficient, and inadequate? Why does He?

7.   How did God use Deborah? Why was she such a good instrument that God could use? (Judges 4 - 5.)

8.   Who was Gideon? What did God teach him? Did God use him in a mighty way? But, what happened to Gideon when his ego (Easing God Out) got in the way?

9.   Even if you are a good person, but there is nothing noteworthy to say about you, what does that mean?

10.   Who puts the "fire" into your spiritual life? Who makes you
        real? Who makes the Bible personal and alive? Who makes
        you confident and courageous about your love for the Lord?

11.   Why is Samson's story sad to the very end? Why should you
        never make Samson a hero? Did he ever become what God
        created him to be? (Judges 13 - 16.)

12.   From I Samuel 1 - 3, what do you know of the last two
        judges of Israel?

13.   What do you love about Hannah?

14.   How big is your influence on your children and
        grandchildren? Humbling, isn't it? So, let's take it seriously
        and work at it.

9

Ruth and Naomi
(and Boaz)

Before we start this chapter, I would like to tell you a personal story. God loves us so much that He tests us. His desire is that through this test, we learn to love and trust Him, and that during this test we run to Him and not away from Him.

After being a singer for over fifty years, I heard the doctor say to me, "Because of a neurological gene, your muscles near your vocal cords are continuously vibrating, causing your voice great distress. I can help you, but you have to decide whether you want to sing or talk. You cannot have both because of the way the treatment works.

Quite a jolt, wouldn't you say? Since I was a child, singing was my life. Of course, I chose to talk, but now we are "talking" big changes in my life. It is like telling a football player that he cannot play, a dancer that she cannot dance, a doctor that he cannot practice, or a teacher that she cannot teach. Singing was what I knew how to do. It was what people knew me for. That was what I thought my worth was based on. Life is not fair. Have you ever said that? Let me tell you right now there are circumstances in our lives that are not going to change. That's just the way it is; so the questions are: "What are you going to do about it?" "How are you going to handle the situation which is not going to go away?"

I believe the answers lie in how well you know the Almighty Sovereign God—how much you truly believe He loves you and has a plan He is working out through you. Do you KNOW that your very creation and existence is for Him and not you? Do you understand that He is really not out for your physical comfort as much as He is trying to change your heart? All of those questions and your answers will have a monumental bearing on how you will react to unexplainable situations and the tribulations of life.

As I have studied the story of Jesus, I have often wondered why one of His disciples denied that he was associated with Jesus, others ran after Jesus' arrest in the garden when the going got tough, and at first none of them would accept that Jesus had risen from the dead. One thing I noticed over and over was that Jesus said many times, "Listen carefully," and then proceeded to tell them His mission was not what they thought it was going to be. He was not going to set up an earthly kingdom, but rather he would die on a cross, and three days later rise from the dead. It was like they didn't want to hear that, and so they didn't. If they had chosen to listen carefully, Jesus explanation would have caused them to understand; therefore, they would have been strong, ready, and prepared, not surprised and spiritually thrown off balance.

The Bible is filled with one "listen carefully" after another, with the goal being to get you and I strong, ready, and prepared, so we are not surprised and spiritually thrown off balance during our lives here.

At my first vocal cord treatment, I remember asking the doctor if I could at least sing at one more concert the next morning because it had been planned for many months. He quickly assured me that I could because the medicine would not begin working until later in the day.

The next morning at 6:00 a.m., I was warming up my singing voice, and it was still strong and powerful. The speaking voice wasn't, but I hadn't had use of that for many months, and I fully believed my mission that morning was to sing. So I was feeling great, and all was on track for one more concert.

Between the time we left our home and arrived at the church an hour and a half later, the medicine had taken hold, but I didn't know it until I opened my mouth to sing the great hymn, "Holy, Holy, Holy, Lord God Almighty." In all my fifty-plus years of singing, I never had trouble finding my pitch; but that morning, I not only couldn't find the pitch, I couldn't even "land" one. I had no control at all. There I was in the front of a church full of people— people who had heard me sing many times, and the reality hit in a split second. Singing, for all intents and purposes, for me was over.

I stopped and began to explain to the audience what was happening. As I was explaining, it dawned on me that I WAS TALKING! Maybe you don't understand, but I had not been able to talk with ease for a long, long time. It had been so long since I got a whole sentence out—and now I was talking complete sentences with no breaking. I looked at my husband, Tom, and his feeling of "horror" look I saw when I had started to sing had changed to a sweet, understanding smile. He heard it, too.

The Lord made it clear in a split second that He had changed my plans and the way I was going to be ministering. I could have looked at the change, fell into self-pity, and missed the journey of a lifetime, or believed with all my heart that He loves me and is in total control of my life—and then watch Him direct my path. *Trust in the LORD with all your heart and lean not on your own understanding; in all your ways acknowledge him, and he will make your paths straight* (Proverbs 3:5-6).

Years of Bible study, in that split second of choice, PAID OFF!

As I continued talking, I became a witness to the Lord doing exactly what He promised—to supply what I needed to fulfill His propose in me. He filled my heart and mind with the Truth of His Word that I had been studying and studying; instead of allowing my human nature to fill that same heart and mind with disappointment and depression. *Do not be anxious about anything, but in everything, by prayer and petition, with thanksgiving, present your requests to God. And the peace of God, which transcends all understanding, will guard your hearts and your minds in Christ Jesus* (Philippians 4:6-7).

That service did not turn out to be a singing concert, but He displayed His power in me with His Words, delivered in the way He wanted (surpassing anything I had planned to do singing). *Now to him who is able to do immeasurably more than all we ask or imagine, according to his power that is at work within us* (Ephesians 3:20). It worked. Of course it worked! That was His plan all along.

So many people today fall into despair, depression, and hopelessness when life is troublesome and unexplainable. You ALWAYS have a choice. You have to fight—I repeat, fight like a warrior, because you are at war with Satan, who is the enemy of your soul and who uses a very powerful, effective, weapon—YOU—your human nature. *For our struggle is not against flesh and blood, but against the rulers, against the authorities, against the powers of this dark world and against the spiritual forces of evil in the heavenly realms* (Ephesians 6:12).

I have experienced too much and believed His Word too much to stop now. So it is with great excitement that I choose to accept this change and to use this twist in my journey to communicate the love of God, and also to honor the seriousness of obeying, trusting, and living out His Word. I now begin tracking the mysterious footsteps of Jesus, your Savior and mine.

Tucked away in the darkest days of the judges, when Israel would fall away from God and worship Baal and other pagan idols, is the precious love story found in the book of Ruth. It's not just a human love story; it is so much more than that. It continues to show God's UNCONDITIONAL love for mankind and His determination to get a Savior to them. Most of the time, He did not have much to work with, so you then see His beautiful way of taking Israel's messes and bringing hope. His love and the orchestration of details in this book are magnificent.

I have mentioned before that God loves us so much that He will do whatever it takes to get our attention when we are either wayward from Him or need a push in our faith. Some of life's hardest crises are a result of His love in action. Not our favorite times, for sure, but if you are willing to look back, you can often see His plan. He DOES know what He is doing. We learned from our study of Judges that Israel was again alienated from the Lord. As we move on to the book of Ruth, we encounter the setting.

In Bethlehem, a sweet little town in Judea, lived the family of Elimelech. He had a wife, Naomi, and two sons. Famine had hit the land in a hard way. Food was very hard to come by. So, like any good father would do, he did what he thought had to be done. MOVE. Move to where he could feed his family. They moved to a pagan country, Moab, about 30-60 miles away, depending on the route taken. What a guy! That's what I thought for a long time. Again, I tend to make heroes out of humans instead of looking at the reality of the situation and the loving hand of God superseding man's bad ideas. It wasn't until I studied the Old Testament in sequence from Genesis to Malachi that I saw God at work to fulfill His mission—Jesus as Savior. And I have arrived at a different perspective of this story than I had previously held. Let's take a look at the story, and I will share my new perspective with you.

Starting with God's promise to Abraham, I watched the evil and disobedience of His treasured possession, the Israelites. Then it goes on through the patriarchs, Moses, Joshua, the judges, and soon the prophets and kings. Many times in the Old Testament, God would hand the Israelites over to their enemies as a result of their disobedience and rebellion. Whoever wrote Psalm 107:4-35 knew the Israelites, their fickle relationship with their God, and testified to God's discipline upon them.

> *4Some wandered in desert wastelands,*
> *finding no way to a city where they could settle.*
> *5They were hungry and thirsty,*
> *and their lives ebbed away.*
> *6Then they cried out to the LORD in their trouble,*
> *and he delivered them from their distress.*
> *7He led them by a straight way*
> *to a city where they could settle.*
> *8Let them give thanks to the LORD for his unfailing love*
> *and his wonderful deeds for men,*
> *9for he satisfies the thirsty*
> *and fills the hungry with good things.*
> *10Some sat in darkness and the deepest gloom,*
> *prisoners suffering in iron chains,*
> *11for they had rebelled against the words of God*
> *and despised the counsel of the Most High.*
> *12So he subjected them to bitter labor;*
> *they stumbled, and there was no one to help.*
> *13Then they cried to the LORD in their trouble,*
> *and he saved them from their distress.*
> *14He brought them out of darkness and the deepest gloom*

and broke away their chains.
15Let them give thanks to the LORD for his
unfailing love
 and his wonderful deeds for men,
16for he breaks down gates of bronze
 and cuts through bars of iron.
17Some became fools through their rebellious ways
 and suffered affliction because of their
iniquities.
18They loathed all food
 and drew near the gates of death.
19Then they cried to the LORD in their trouble,
 and he saved them from their distress.
20He sent forth his word and healed them;
 he rescued them from the grave.
21Let them give thanks to the LORD for his
unfailing love
 and his wonderful deeds for men.
22Let them sacrifice thank offerings
 and tell of his works with songs of joy.
23Others went out on the sea in ships;
 they were merchants on the mighty waters.
24They saw the works of the LORD,
 his wonderful deeds in the deep.
25For he spoke and stirred up a tempest
 that lifted high the waves.
26They mounted up to the heavens and went down to
the depths;
 in their peril their courage melted away.
27They reeled and staggered like drunken men;
 they were at their wits' end.
28Then they cried out to the LORD in their trouble,
 and he brought them out of their distress.
29He stilled the storm to a whisper;
 the waves of the sea were hushed.
30They were glad when it grew calm,

and he guided them to their desired haven.
31Let them give thanks to the LORD for his
unfailing love
    and his wonderful deeds for men.
32Let them exalt him in the assembly of the people
    and praise him in the council of the elders.
33He turned rivers into a desert,
    flowing springs into thirsty ground,
34and fruitful land into a salt waste,
    because of the wickedness of those who lived
there.
35He turned the desert into pools of water
    and the parched ground into flowing springs;

Did you notice their pattern? They went their own way, God sent a crisis, they cried out to Him, He forgave them, and then the cycle started all over again. The verse I really want to emphasize is verse 33; *He turned rivers into a desert, flowing springs into thirsty ground....* That sounds like a famine to me. We just assume that Bethlehem was experiencing a famine because it didn't rain. Well, Who controls the rain? This famine was deliberate to again get the attention of the disobedient Israelites—the people He adored.

"'I will break down your stubborn pride and make
the sky above you like iron and the ground beneath
you like bronze. Your strength will be spent in vain,
because your soil will not yield its crops, nor will
the trees of the land yield their fruit.'"
(Leviticus 26:19-20.)

The sky over your head will be bronze, the ground
beneath you iron. The LORD will turn the rain of
your country into dust and powder; it will come
down from the skies until you are destroyed.
(Deuteronomy 28:23-24.)

Sometimes I have looked at the Israelites repetitive disobedience and wondered why they were so dense. Couldn't they see what they were doing? Couldn't they remember that just yesterday God was sufficient? Didn't they learn from the last time? Then I realized that my questions rang a loud bell in my ear. It's so easy to follow that sad pattern. I know I have failed to see what I was doing, chose not to remember that God was sufficient yesterday, and, no, I guess I didn't learn either. No wonder one of my favorite songs is, "Great is Thy Faithfulness...morning by morning new mercies I see." He IS so faithful, so patient, and so full of mercy and grace.

The Lord was going to use this famine to cause them to fall to their knees, see their need, and cry out to Him for His forgiveness. So do you really think that the Lord's plan for the Elimelech family was to hightail it to a pagan country? Of course not! You can't run from God! You can't run from your problems! His intent was for them to face up to their failures and confess their sins. The whole town of Bethlehem didn't up and move. Many stayed and watched the Lord provide. They were the ones who chose to see God's purpose, and they trusted Him.

Just what happens to a family who becomes a part of another culture, style, religion, and society? I'm certain that Elimelech had to get work among the Moabites, and as his sons grew older, he shoved them right into that same work force and environment, too. That's pretty obvious, because the boys married Moabite women. After several years, Moab became home to the guys. I say "the guys" because I don't think that it ever became home to Naomi. I personally don't think Naomi ever wanted to leave Bethlehem. She knew her God. He never wants us to run from Him, but rather run to Him in repentance. She got the message. But I don't think she had much of a choice. Elimelech could take her out of Bethlehem, but he couldn't take her God out of her heart, so her God went right with her to this pagan country. Your faith goes where you go. I think of people like Cory TenBoom who were in the concentration camps. It was their faith that went with them which kept them going day after day in those awful camps. When you can't see an end to your situation, and despair, defeat, discouragement, depression, and delusion want to set in, it is your faith that will raise you out of your dark pit. Faith and faith alone! When faith is all you have, that is when you find that it is enough. What is faith? It is simply how much you know and trust your God.

When Naomi met her new daughters-in-law, I am sure that it broke her heart. She knew God's rules about marriage to non-Israelites. ✞ She knew there would be consequences. She could have turned on them. She could have chosen to have nothing to do with them. Imagine what kind of home environment that would have been! She chose to love them the way God loved her—unconditionally. She couldn't change the situation, but God's love was in her heart. Out of that kind of love, when the men were out working, one would suspect she chose to teach her girls through the Word and through her testimony (testifying to what she knew). Her actions painted such a beautiful picture of the character of her God that the girls fell in love with their God-fearing mother-in-law.

As you know, many "in-law" relationships are not easy. It takes effort and a lot of give, patience, understanding, and stepping aside to make it work. I am not going to go into that any farther, because I think you know what I mean. And Naomi was willing to show God's love in such a way that those girls were never the same.

Elimelech and their two sons died—first her husband, and then years later, both of her sons. What a loss! It's beyond devastating. I can't even imagine her pain. When we are in this kind of excruciating pain, it is so, so easy to let our emotions get bigger than our faith. Emotions are very powerful. We mentioned anger when we studied Moses, but grief is another strong emotion that can take you down, and you think that you can't ever get up. This is exactly what happened to Naomi. She didn't lose her faith, but her grief took over and pushed her faith aside. Bitterness and sadness took over, and she lost her hope. It's when we are down to this extent that Satan comes charging in with all his ammunition—those "d" words that I mentioned just a bit ago. You talk about a dark, slimy pit! That's just what you feel like you're in when you lose your hope.

Naomi heard, even in Moab, how God provided for His people in Bethlehem. With that new information, she decided she was going home! She and the girls set out, but then along the way, Naomi had a talk with them and basically released them from her family to go back and find new husbands and start their families. Both girls wouldn't hear of it! They wept and said they wanted to go with her. Now, think about it, we're talking about their MOTHER-IN-LAW! Naomi tried to reason with them; and finally, Orpah turned and went back.

> *But Ruth replied, "Don't urge me to leave you or to turn back from you. Where you go I will go, and where you stay I will stay. Your people will be my people and your God my God. Where you die I will die, and there I will be buried. May the LORD deal with me, be it ever so severely, if anything but death separates you and me"* (Ruth 1:16-17).

Ruth was willing to leave all that was comfortable and familiar. It's like she knew she had to follow the Lord, believing that His will is better than any worldly comfort. Naomi realized that Ruth meant business, so she stopped urging her to go back. It certainly looks like God honored Naomi's faith and testimony through those difficult years in Moab. Naomi's faith was hanging by a thread at this point, but it was there. They traveled together in their journey back to Bethlehem.

When they arrived in Bethlehem, the whole town was stirred. *"Can this be Naomi?"* they asked. They still recognized her after all those years. But she was in no mood to rekindle warm, fuzzy, relationships.

> *"Don't call me Naomi," she told them. "Call me Mara, because the Almighty has made my life very bitter. I went away full, but the LORD has brought me back empty. Why call me Naomi? The LORD has afflicted me; the Almighty has brought misfortune upon me"* (1:20-21).

Now that's bitterness! How come God always gets the blame, when He gave the commands and warned of the consequences? We blame Him, when all along it's our own fault. But who wants to see that, right? It's so much easier to blame God and expect Him to bail us out of our own doing.

When you read the short four chapters of Ruth, you can't miss God's perfect, spit-second timing. I don't know if you use the words "lucky" or "coincidence," but if you really believe in God's providence, those words should really be omitted from your vocabulary. We are not lucky people; we are blessed people to be in the Plan and the Hand of an Almighty God.

When did Naomi and Ruth get into Bethlehem? Right at barley time. The drama began. The Lord was now going to start to turn all things out for good. His Son's line WAS going to continue.

When Naomi and Ruth came back to Bethlehem, they came with nothing, and there probably was no home to go to, either. After Naomi let them all have it with her bitter attitude, it doesn't seem that anyone invited them over for dinner or to be overnight guests either. They also might not have liked it that Naomi had a pagan daughter-in-law. Whatever the reason, Naomi and Ruth were on their own. It looked pretty bleak. Ruth had noticed that in the barley fields there were gleaners. Gleaning was Israel's welfare program. Owners allowed the poorest of the poor to pick up leftover grain behind the harvesters. We are now really starting to see the heart of Ruth—her character. Character is different than personality. We all have different personalities. They make us unique. We are like snowflakes. Not one of us is the same. He created us with different personalities; but His plan is that we all have the same character—the character of His Son. Those characteristics are the Fruit of His Spirit: Love, Joy, Peace, Patience, Kindness, Goodness, Faithfulness, Gentleness, and Self-control. Those qualities make us Christ-like. A very worthwhile goal to have!

Ruth was willing to put her pride aside and glean in the fields to supply food for her mother-in-law. It was terribly hard work, too. But you never hear a complaint or whine from her. She does what has to be done. The apostle Paul had good advice to the Philippians in chapter 2:14-15:

> *Do everything without complaining or arguing, so that you may become blameless and pure, children of God without fault in a crooked and depraved generation, in which you shine like stars in the universe....*

Have you ever felt embarrassed to do a job or perform a service because you thought it was beneath you? Paul says in Colossians 3:23-24:

Whatever you do, work at it with all your heart, as working for the Lord, not for men, since you know that you will receive an inheritance from the Lord as a reward. It is the Lord Christ you are serving.

That says it as plain as can be, don't you think?

With God's plan in full motion, Ruth landed in the field of Boaz. Boaz was one of the Israelites who obeyed God, stayed put in Bethlehem, and learned from His discipline. The Lord blessed Him. Boaz had land and employees. He treated them with respect, and they returned it. It was a great working environment. People think that to have a working environment like that today is impossible. Remember, nothing is impossible if God is at the center. Actually, I should say if God is the Boss! That will always be the key.

It didn't take Boaz long to notice Ruth gleaning in his field. He inquired of his foreman, *"Whose young woman is that?"* (2:5b.) He found out that she was a Moabite and a hard worker. He also found out about her love for her mother-in-law, and he saw her beauty inside and out. I always pictured her to be gorgeous and Boaz to be very handsome. They might have been, but I think we see their godly character, and that will ALWAYS come out on our faces as beautiful.   That beauty radiates through the wrinkles, past the blemishes and flaws, extra weight, glasses, braces, deformities, and handicaps. Yes, the heart of Christ's character is BEAUTIFUL. That's all there is to it! We have two beautiful characters that the Lord was using here. He sure knew how to pick 'em!

Boaz invited her to have some bread with his servant girls, and he asked the harvesters to pull extra stalks out for her, and do it in a way that wouldn't embarrass her. So when Ruth got home that night with all that grain, Naomi was shocked and asked her where she had gleaned. When Ruth told her, everything changed. The ugly scales of bitterness fell off her spiritual eyes. She saw the Lord's hand again. He hadn't left her. She had left Him. Naomi was

BACK! Boaz was a relative. Naomi got her hope back. Life is pointless without hope. But with hope we can get through it all, because our Hope is Jesus, and He will never disappoint us.

The details about how the Lord brought this couple together are better than any romance novel, because in the middle of their love was obedience to the Lord, the desire to do His will, trust to believe that His plan was perfect, and wanting nothing less. Boaz waited on the Lord and did nothing in haste or by impulse.

So after following proper protocol, Boaz took Ruth as his wife. She conceived and had a son. Boaz and Ruth became the great grandparents of King David—twenty-eight generations later, and from this very line, came Jesus, the Savior. God could not have chosen two better people. They had the hearts for it, and to get the kind of hearts the Lord could use took hard times, challenges, selflessness, and the willingness to be molded into the people whom God could use. If you want to be known as one who is willing to be a vessel the Lord can use, you had better mean it and want it bad, because it doesn't come easy. But if these two could come out of this book, I believe they would not hesitate to proclaim that it was worth it all.

What did God mold this pagan Moabite into? The Proverbs 31 woman! He took away her title of being a pagan Moabite and changed her into one of God's children. God gives every woman great potential, ability, and godly power if we entrust our lives to Him. Read these words in 31:10-31:

10 A wife of noble character who can find?
        She is worth far more than rubies.
11 Her husband has full confidence in her
        and lacks nothing of value.
12 She brings him good, not harm,
        all the days of her life.
13 She selects wool and flax
        and works with eager hands.
14 She is like the merchant ships,
        bringing her food from afar.
15 She gets up while it is still dark;

she provides food for her family
and portions for her servant girls.
16*She considers a field and buys it;*
out of her earnings she plants a vineyard.
17*She sets about her work vigorously;*
her arms are strong for her tasks.
18*She sees that her trading is profitable,*
and her lamp does not go out at night.
19*In her hand she holds the distaff*
and grasps the spindle with her fingers.
20*She opens her arms to the poor*
and extends her hands to the needy.
21*When it snows, she has no fear for her household;*
for all of them are clothed in scarlet.
22*She makes coverings for her bed;*
she is clothed in fine linen and purple.
23*Her husband is respected at the city gate,*
where he takes his seat among the elders of the land.
24*She makes linen garments and sells them,*
and supplies the merchants with sashes.
25*She is clothed with strength and dignity;*
she can laugh at the days to come.
26*She speaks with wisdom,*
and faithful instruction is on her tongue.
27*She watches over the affairs of her household*
and does not eat the bread of idleness.
28*Her children arise and call her blessed;*
her husband also, and he praises her:
29*"Many women do noble things,*
but you surpass them all."
30*Charm is deceptive, and beauty is fleeting;*
but a woman who fears the LORD is to be praised.
31*Give her the reward she has earned,*
and let her works bring her praise at the city gate.

Did you notice that she is a whole package? Let me try to list this proverb in today's language:

1. She trusts and loves.
2. She encourages and lives her life as an example. She's not moody.
3. She doesn't cause the family financial hardship.
4. She is not afraid to work hard and long to do whatever it takes, and she does it with the right attitude.
5. She thinks things through. She's not impulsive.
6. She is careful with her free time.
7. She is compassionate.
8. She is prepared. She thinks ahead and does not procrastinate.
9. She is not an embarrassment to her family or friends.
10. She is classy and dresses modestly.
11. She is SURE of the future.
12. She thinks before she speaks.
13. She fears the Lord and seeks His will.
14. Those who know her best, praise her most.

When you look at a list like that, it looks like a big a mountain to climb, and you just don't believe you have what it takes to get there. Well, you are correct. No woman has what it takes to be all that. The Holy Spirit is just waiting to take over when we are willing to step aside and let HIM accomplish it all through us. He can and will get us to the top. Yes, it's a hard climb, but if you are willing to recognize and remind yourself of what He has done for you, somehow the desire to allow the Spirit to take over and get us to the top is such a proper way to say thank You. He's worth it!

Ruth was beautiful. But I think there was one more reason why Boaz was drawn to her. Remember, I asked you to remember Boaz when he was mentioned earlier in our study. God had started to prepare this union already in the book of Joshua. Rahab was Boaz's mother. There had to have been a time when Rahab sat her little boy down and told him a true story. A story about herself. A story of God's love and forgiveness. How only He could take her, a prostitute, and engraft her into the family of God. ✞ I feel sure that

Boaz adored his mother. Seeing her humility, and watching her flourish in her faith with the kind of past she had, I believe helped him see in Ruth the same kind of life-changing miracle, and he didn't want to miss being a part of that. Allowing God to erase your past and to use your new life in Him can only mean REAL LIVING!

CHAPTER 9

JESUS'   SIGNPOSTS

"Non-Israelites": Pg. 199

● ...Acts 11:17-18, *So if God gave them the same gift as he gave us, who believed in the Lord Jesus Christ, who was I to think that I could oppose God?" When they heard this, they had no further objections and praised God, saying, "So then, God has granted even the Gentiles repentance unto life."*

● ...Romans 15:16-17, *to be a minister of Christ Jesus to the Gentiles with the priestly duty of proclaiming the gospel of God, so that the Gentiles might become an offering acceptable to God, sanctified by the Holy Spirit. Therefore I glory in Christ Jesus in my service to God.*

"Family of God": Pg. 205

● ...Matthew 1:5-6, *Salmon the father of Boaz, whose mother was Rahab, Boaz the father of Obed, whose mother was Ruth, Obed the father of Jesse, and Jesse the father of King David.*

Lesson 9: Ruth and Naomi (and Boaz)
Ruth 1 - 4

1. When did this story take place?

2. What were the conditions in Israel at that time?

3. Why do you think that there was a famine? (Psalm 107.) What have you been learning about when it comes to the consequences of disobedience and turning away from God?

4. A reminder: What does God intend to happen to you when He disciplines? Does He ever want you to run from Him and feel self-sufficient to fix whatever the problem? Can you run from God? Can you hide? Are you really able to be self-sufficient?

5. What can happen when you adopt another culture?

6. When Naomi moved with her family, what did she take with her that showed itself through her daughters-in-law? What kind of mother-in-law was she to those pagan women?

7. What happened to Naomi when her husband and sons died? What is the danger when feelings get bigger than your faith?

8. When do you believe that Naomi's faith got back into first place?

9. Why was Ruth willing to leave all that was familiar and comfortable and go to Bethlehem with Naomi?

10. How did God honor Ruth's faithfulness to Naomi and to Him?

11.   Who was Boaz? Who was his mother? (Matthew1:5.) What
        do you think that she told her son of her past? Do you think
        Boaz's mother's story played a part in his godly character and
        how he looked at Ruth, the Moabite?

12.   What is a testimony? What is yours? Is it affecting and
        influencing others around you?

13.   Can YOU be a Proverbs 31 woman? How?

14.   What does the story of Ruth teach you, personally?

10

The First Three Kings of Israel

It's so hard to leave the faith of Naomi and the sweet love and obedience story of Ruth and Boaz, but we have to continue on and watch the Lord fulfill His mission. We have to go back to the nation of Israel—to their never ending battle with rebellion against their God, who chose them as His own, delivered them from bondage, supplied their every need, and loved them unconditionally. It was like they enjoyed smacking Him in the face. And what did He do in return? He disciplined and loved them back into a right relationship. But it never lasted. They always thought they knew better. That IS the struggle. It always has been, and it will be until we get to glory. SELF! It's ugly. It's selfish. It hurts others as well as us. It will never win. It will always suffer consequences, and yet we still think that we know better than God. I stand amazed at our stupidity; and I stand amazed at God's love, patience, grace and mercy.

I remember during my later teens, when I was really so much smarter than my parents (just kidding, Mom and Dad, but I really thought so then), my dad gave me strict instructions to come right home after school and NOT to go see my boyfriend. I had Dad's good car, and I heard the instructions. They were not too difficult to understand, but I wanted my own way and thought I could do what I wanted. After school, I went to where my boyfriend Tom was staying, thinking I could get home before my dad even knew. But when I got back into my car to go home, the battery was dead. Not too big of a problem, because Tom found jumper cables. The problem came when he put them on the battery wrong and the battery blew up—acid everywhere. Then, to make matters worse, Tom and I got into an argument, because instead of caring whether Tom was seriously injured, I cared first about what my dad was going to say.

My dad never got mad quickly. But when he finally did, HE DID, and I knew it. I was scared to death to call him. We were right by Tom's sister's house, so I asked his sister's husband if he would call my dad and tell him what had happened. He did it! My dad was very cool about it. But he also slowly told him that I was not to come home that night, that he would come into town in the morning and put a new battery in, and that I was just to go to school the next day. He needed time before he saw me again. I didn't have a change of clothes or anything because I certainly had not planned to spend the night with Tom's sister and brother-in-law. They were gracious to let me stay. She gave me a pair of her pajamas to wear, and I wore the same clothes to school the next morning.

I dreaded the time when school was over and I had to sheepishly make my way home. When I saw my dad, he didn't yell and scream; but I knew that I had disappointed him, and that's what hurt the most. I could take any punishment, but I knew I had hurt him by disobeying. That was one time I learned my lesson well. That's the thing, we can learn from our mistakes. They can teach us a lot! But it seemed like with the Israelites, that they just would not learn from theirs.

At the end of Judges, we read that everyone did as they saw fit. Basically, they all did what they jolly-well wanted to. Chaos! Left to man, we would hang ourselves out to dry on this world's secular-leaning clothesline. That is why the Lord gave us the Ten Commandments. They are like a spiritual leash around our necks. We wander, and the Lord cuts us a little slack; but when we wander too far, He will give it a yank and pull us back. Oh, we are a pathetic people on our own, and does the Lord ever know it! That's why He was so determined to get our Savior here. He is our only way of redemption.

The elders of Israel went to Samuel and said they wanted a king just like all the other nations had. The other nations were pagan, and they wanted to follow their influence? What were they thinking? Samuel was very displeased, but he went to the Lord, and the Lord gave him these words in I Samuel 8:7-9:

And the LORD told him: "Listen to all that the people are saying to you; it is not you they have rejected, but they have rejected me as their king. As they have done from the day I brought them up out of Egypt until this day, forsaking me and serving other gods, so they are doing to you. Now listen to them; but warn them solemnly and let them know what the king who will reign over them will do." ☩

How sad! They had the ultimate King, who was God and He was able to give them whatever was needed and necessary, but they wanted an earthly king. That's why God told Samuel to warn them that this human king would disappoint them because he would be selfish and also very unable to be their all in all. But the people refused to listen and demanded a king. The Lord told Samuel that if they think they know better, *"Listen to them and give them a king"* (I Samuel 8:22b).

The Lord guided Samuel to Saul, a Benjamite. He was an impressive young man. He stood a head taller than any of the others. He was without equal among the Israelites. Yes, he looked kingly. But looks can be deceiving. You would think they would have had a glimpse of his character when, after he was chosen and Samuel asked where he was, he was found hiding among the baggage. They now had a king, but he was a scaredy cat. Oh my, what a way to start! Saul was thirty years old when he became king, and he reigned over Israel forty-two years. During his reign, he failed to obey the Lord's commands, and he was told by Samuel that when his reign was over, his family would not continue to rule; the Lord had already picked the next king. He had sought out a man after His own heart. What a low blow! Saul started to change after that, because the Spirit of the Lord had departed from Saul, and an evil spirit from the Lord tormented him (I Samuel 16:14). What was this evil spirit the Lord sent? Perhaps Saul went into a state of deep depression, or perhaps after the Holy Spirit had left Saul, God allowed an evil demon to torment him as judgment for his disobedience. Either way, Saul was driven to suicide.

> *Saul said to his armor-bearer, "Draw your sword*
> *and run me through, or these uncircumcised*
> *fellows will come and run me through and abuse*
> *me"* (1 Samuel 31:4).

In the meantime, God had Samuel anoint the next king so that He could start getting him prepared. This time, the Lord said to Samuel in I Samuel 16:7b:

> *"Do not consider his appearance or his height, for I*
> *have rejected him. The LORD does not look at the*
> *things man looks at. Man looks at the outward*
> *appearance, but the LORD looks at the heart."*

So when Samuel went to the house of Jesse and, one by one, his sons came through the line for his approval, God kept saying no. Samuel was probably confused, because God had told him that the next king would come from this family. He finally just came out and asked if these were all the sons he had. Jesse said that his youngest was tending sheep, and he was out in the fields. They went out to the fields and retrieved David.

> *So Samuel took the horn of oil and anointed him in*
> *the presence of his brothers, and from that day on*
> *the Spirit of the LORD came upon David in power.*
> *Samuel then went to Ramah* (I Samuel 16:13).

David was very talented. Not only was he a shepherd, but he could play the harp and write poetry. He was known in the community as a brave man and a warrior. He could speak well, was good looking, and it was noticeable that the Lord was with him (I Samuel 16:18). I love that line—it was noticeable that the Lord was with him. On a day that Saul was in a bad state of mind, his attendants brought David into the palace to play for Saul. Saul liked him very much, and David became one of his armor bearers. Saul asked David's father if David could now remain in his service. The way the Lord places people onto their next stepping stone of His plan is the best. God works behind the scenes WAY before we even see it.

When this little girl was standing against the school wall being picked last every day, the Lord was there. When this little girl grew up and didn't make the team, the Lord was there. When the boy she loved and thought loved her back, didn't, the Lord was there. When she didn't get the job, the Lord was there. When a serious problem came in her marriage, the Lord was there building her character and proving He is who He says He is. Building our character takes time. Molding us into the person He created us to be takes time. Preparing us for the mission He has called us out to do for Him takes time. It also takes some hard knocks. That part is the hardest, but God does His best work when He has us so humbled that we throw up our arms and finally say, "Whatever You want, Lord." That is where He wants us.

I never saw David buck God's plan—taking him out of the shepherd's field into the house of Saul. No objections, just obedience. God knew this was a man after His own heart. David was a willing piece of clay, ready to be molded. That's something to think about, right? How willing are we to be molded, or are we going into His process kicking and screaming? Remember, it's only in His will that we find true satisfaction, contentment, and confidence, so why the kicking and screaming, anyway? It really doesn't make any sense when we act like that. The Psalmist says it EXACTLY right when describing how the Lord wants us to come to Him when deciding which way our heart is going—our way or His: *Teach me to do your will, for you are my God; may your good Spirit lead me on level ground* (Psalm 143:10).

That's probably why the Psalmist was David. He learned to seek God's will, and believe me, he knew the difference. David wasn't perfect. He knew he had flaws and weaknesses. He learned that his way got him into trouble, but when he was in the center of God's will, all his flaws and weaknesses were replaced with the Lord's strength and power.

One of Israel's toughest and constant enemies was the Philistines. They were a crude bunch. One of their team players was named Goliath. He was over nine feet tall. His appearance was chilling, and his shield bearer always went ahead of him. Goliath was a Philistine bully, and he loved the position. He would come out twice daily and challenge anyone to fight him. Every time he would shout this out, all the Israelites were terrified. Again, just as the Lord would have it, and in His perfect timing, David's father told David to check on his brothers who had followed Saul to the war and then report back so he would know how they were doing. Israel was at war with the Philistines, and like any father, he was concerned how his boys were doing. When David got there, Goliath stepped out to do one of his scare tactics. This time David took him on. He calmly said to this giant:

> *"You come against me with sword and spear and javelin, but I come against you in the name of the* LORD *Almighty, the God of the armies of Israel, whom you have defied. This day the* LORD *will hand you over to me, and I'll strike you down and cut off your head. Today I will give the carcasses of the Philistine army to the birds of the air and the beasts of the earth, and the whole world will know that there is a God in Israel. All those gathered here will know that it is not by sword or spear that the* LORD *saves; for the battle is the* LORD's, *and he will give all of you into our hands"* (I Samuel 17:45b-47).

Now that's confidence in his Lord. David reached into his bag, took out a stone, slung it, and struck the Philistine on the forehead. The giant went tumbling down. David then took out his sword and cut Goliath's head off.

The Israelites were ecstatic! The bully was dead! David was a hero! I Samuel 18:7 says, *As they danced, they sang: "Saul has slain his thousands, and David his tens of thousands."*

That didn't set well with Saul. The green-eyed monster took over. Jealousy is nasty, and Saul played right into that monster's hand. It grew to the point where Saul wanted David DEAD! He tried a number of times to kill him, but the Lord had plans for David. That should give us such comfort! Instead of worrying about our future, that story reminds us that nothing will happen in our lives unless God says so, and only when HIS plan for us is accomplished.

So we will not die a minute early or a minute late (Psalm 139:16). His appointments with us are right on time, and our death is an appointment with Him, and Him alone. Job says that it's the Lord who gives life, and the Lord who takes life. So there! That's settled.

We mentioned before that even though David was a man after God's own heart, he still came with flaws. One of his biggest flaws, just like with Moses, was anger. David was a superior warrior and commander of an army of men. Before he became king, he and the mighty men needed some food and drink while in the fields. They met up with Nabal. David remembered that he once had given Nabal's men hospitality when they needed it, so he thought this would work out fine. David's men asked Nabal for the favor, and Nabal acted like he had never heard of David and said no. The negative answer got back to David and he went ballistic—livid! Mad isn't even close to David's emotion. His anger was out of control, and he vowed to kill every male in the household of Nabal. He told his men to put on their swords because he was out for blood. Abigail, Nabal's beautiful and very intelligent wife, got wind of this and lost no time in getting everything ready to avoid this pending blood bath. Loaded down with ample supplies, she rode off to meet David. When Abigail saw David, she quickly got off her donkey and bowed down before him. She totally took the blame, and the Lord used her to quicken David's senses before it was too late. Listen to her God-given words to David in I Samuel 25:26-31:

"Now since the LORD has kept you, my master, from bloodshed and from avenging yourself with your own hands, as surely as the LORD lives and as you live, may your enemies and all who intend to harm my master be like Nabal. And let this gift, which your servant has brought to my master, be given to the men who follow you. Please forgive your servant's offense, for the LORD will certainly make a lasting dynasty for my master, because he fights the LORD's battles. Let no wrongdoing be found in you as long as you live. Even though someone is pursuing you to take your life, the life of my master will be bound securely in the bundle of the living by

the LORD your God. But the lives of your enemies he will hurl away as from the pocket of a sling. When the LORD has done for my master every good thing he promised concerning him and has appointed him leader over Israel, my master will not have on his conscience the staggering burden of needless bloodshed or of having avenged himself. And when the LORD has brought my master success, remember your servant."

That perfectly spoken speech went directly to David's heart without condemnation, and David received the message loud and clear. David praised the Lord for Abigail and for saving him from doing what he would have been so sorry for later, because he was acting with uncontrollable anger. Abigail went home to confess to her husband what she had done and to face this fool. In I Samuel 25:25b, Abigail herself said of Nabal, *"He is just like his name—his name is Fool, and folly goes with him."* Psalm 14:1a says, *The fool says in his heart, "There is no God."* So calling him a fool was far more serious than just name calling.

God stepped in, Nabal's heart failed him, and he became like a stone. About ten days later, the Lord struck Nabal and he died. I wondered how come the Lord gave Nabal ten days before He struck him dead. Knowing the love and patience of our Lord, I wouldn't be a bit surprised if the Lord gave Nabal ten days to repent and come clean; but apparently this surly, mean man ran out of chances.

The Lord loves a good love story. Here is another one. Abigail became David's wife. The Lord knows exactly what to do, always.

David became quite the conquering warrior. In II Samuel 2, he became king, first over the kingdom of Judah, and then later over the whole kingdom of Israel. What happens to humans, more often than not, and even to the best of God's people, is that pride sets in. Even when it has been God all along, man starts to take the credit and starts to puff up with selfish pride. In II Samuel 11, David fell, and he fell hard. His root problem, or sin, in this chapter was disobedience. He was supposed to be with his men in battle, but instead he stayed back. He probably was bored, or had too much time on his hands. One evening David was walking around on the roof of his palace, and his eyes started wandering. He spotted Bathsheba bathing. He liked and wanted what he saw, and after all, he was king, so who was going to stop him? So he called for her to be brought to his bed. She became pregnant; and now they had a huge problem, because she was married to Uriah, who was fighting in the battle and was NOT home. There was now no denying whose baby it was. In short order, David compounded his sin by putting Uriah on the front line, where he was killed. David was now an adulterer and a murderer. Yes, he was a man after God's own heart; but self took over, and the Lord was very displeased with him. David became cold and hard to all that had happened. Then the Lord sent a man named Nathan to confront David by using this story:

> The LORD sent Nathan to David. When he came to him, he said, "There were two men in a certain town, one rich and the other poor. The rich man had a very large number of sheep and cattle, but the poor man had nothing except one little ewe lamb he had bought. He raised it, and it grew up with him and his children. It shared his food, drank from his cup and even slept in his arms. It was like a daughter to him.
>
> "Now a traveler came to the rich man, but the rich man refrained from taking one of his own sheep or cattle to prepare a meal for the traveler who had come to him. Instead, he took the ewe lamb that belonged to the poor man and prepared it for the one who had come to him."
>
> David burned with anger against the man and said to Nathan, "As surely as the LORD lives, the man who did this deserves to die! He must pay for that lamb four times over, because he did such a thing and had no pity."
>
> Then Nathan said to David, "You are the man!..." (2 Samuel 12:1-7a.)

David confessed, and his sin was forgiven. But because of what he had done, he had made the enemies of the Lord show utter contempt. He, a man of God, totally blew it while the world watched. Let's follow David's pattern here. 2 Samuel 11:1 reveals:

> *In the spring, at the time when kings go off to war, David sent Joab out with the king's men and the whole Israelite army. They destroyed the Ammonites and besieged Rabbah. But David remained in Jerusalem.*

If he had been where he should have been, none of this would have happened. Instead of being on the battlefield, David was home in bed. From verse 11:2a, we read, *One evening David got up from his bed and walked around on the roof of the palace.*

Do you suppose the reason David couldn't sleep was because he should have been out with his men leading them in battle? Here the opportunity presented itself. It started with lusting. In verse 11:2b, we read. *From the roof he saw a woman bathing. The woman was very beautiful.* It continued with him acting out that lustful desire. In verse 11:3-4, we read:

> *and David sent someone to find out about her. The man said, "Isn't this Bathsheba, the daughter of Eliam and the wife of Uriah the Hittite?" Then David sent messengers to get her. She came to him, and he slept with her. (She had purified herself from her uncleanness.) Then she went back home.*

And then came the result of that sinful act in 11:5, *The woman conceived and sent word to David, saying, "I am pregnant."*

And then in panic, David had to "fix" the results of his sinful action. We read of David's atrocious behavior toward Bathsheba's husband Uriah in 11:15, *In it he wrote, "Put Uriah in the front line where the fighting is fiercest. Then withdraw from him so he will be struck down and die."*

Can you see it? Sin's spiraling staircase, leading you down step by step. See how fast sin leads you lower and lower into the depths of self indulgence? All this from David, whom God had referred to in 1 Samuel 13:14:

> *"But now your kingdom will not endure; the* LORD *has sought out a man after his own heart and appointed him leader of his people, because you have not kept the* LORD*'s command."*

So do take heed and learn from David to stay in Christ and away from that sinful spiraling staircase. Remember, in the Ten Commandments we are told not to misuse His name. Because David thought his name was more important than God's, even for just one night, there were serious consequences. The baby that Bathsheba bore died. It was a horrible time. David's family would never have peace in it again. But out of the overflow of David's brokenness, he wrote some of the Psalms that are still beloved today, for example, Psalm 51:1-17. Hear his heart:

> *1Have mercy on me, O God,*
> *   according to your unfailing love;*
> *   according to your great compassion*
> *   blot out my transgressions.*
> *2Wash away all my iniquity*
> *   and cleanse me from my sin.*
> *3For I know my transgressions,*
> *   and my sin is always before me.*
> *4Against you, you only, have I sinned*
> *   and done what is evil in your sight,*
> *   so that you are proved right when you speak*
> *   and justified when you judge.*
> *5Surely I was sinful at birth,*
> *   sinful from the time my mother conceived me.*
> *6Surely you desire truth in the inner parts;*
> *   you teach me wisdom in the inmost place.*
> *7Cleanse me with hyssop, and I will be clean;*

wash me, and I will be whiter than snow.
8Let me hear joy and gladness;
let the bones you have crushed rejoice.
9Hide your face from my sins
and blot out all my iniquity.
10Create in me a pure heart, O God,
and renew a steadfast spirit within me.
11Do not cast me from your presence
or take your Holy Spirit from me.
12Restore to me the joy of your salvation
and grant me a willing spirit, to sustain me.
13Then I will teach transgressors your ways,
and sinners will turn back to you.
14Save me from bloodguilt,
O God, the God who saves me,
and my tongue will sing of your righteousness.
15O Lord, open my lips,
and my mouth will declare your praise.
16You do not delight in sacrifice, or I would bring it;
you do not take pleasure in burnt offerings.
17The sacrifices of God are a broken spirit;
a broken and contrite heart,
O God, you will not despise.

David took Bathsheba as his wife. After their first child died, she bore him another child. This child was Solomon ✞, and he became the next king. Even after all that had happened, you still see Bathsheba in the line of Christ. Our God, so full of compassion and forgiveness, used flawed people to get His beloved Son to this earth. In I Kings 2:2-4, David gave this charge to Solomon:

"I am about to go the way of all the earth," he said. "So be strong, show yourself a man, and observe what the LORD your God requires: Walk in his ways, and keep his decrees and commands, his laws and requirements, as written in the Law of Moses, so that you may prosper in all you do and

wherever you go, and that the LORD may keep his
promise to me: `If your descendants watch how
they live, and if they walk faithfully before me with
all their heart and soul, you will never fail to have
a man on the throne of Israel.'"

Good advice from the old man. Too bad he hadn't listened
with both of his own ears.

The Lord appeared to Solomon during the night in a dream
and told him that He would give him whatever he asked for.
Solomon, knowing the huge responsibility of the throne, requested
wisdom. The Lord was pleased with what Solomon asked for, and
He not only gave him wisdom and discernment, but also great riches
and honor. Solomon became known throughout the world for his
wisdom and riches. Nations and leaders were awed by his God-given
gifts and abilities.

The greatest achievement in Solomon's reign was the
building of God's temple. And after that project, it seemed like it
was a downward spiral for Solomon. Granted, he was greater in
riches and wisdom than all the other kings of the earth; the whole
world sought audience with Solomon to hear the wisdom God had
put in his heart. Everyone would bring him gifts, and that just added
to his treasury. With all his wealth, plus the addition of women to
the equation (lots of women); Solomon was heading for big trouble.
He especially loved foreign women, women with whom God
commanded they not intermarry because these foreign women would
bring with them their foreign gods. He would be susceptible to
having his heart redirected towards their gods instead of the One
God. He knew the command; but nevertheless, Solomon did what
Solomon wanted. He had seven hundred wives of royal birth and
three hundred concubines, and his wives DID lead him astray. With
that kind of attitude and lifestyle, the Lord became very angry with
Solomon, because his heart had turned away from the Lord, the God
of Israel. And, in turn, God tore the kingdom away from him.

During Solomon's life, and with the wisdom God had given
him, he wrote the book of Proverbs. It contains amazing and
practical truths for life. But later, when his life took a dive because
of his pride, he wrote Ecclesiastes to show his folly, where it took

him in his thoughts, and the lessons he learned. He takes us on his journey of life, explaining with such strong language that, *"Meaningless! Meaningless!" says the Teacher. "Utterly meaningless! Everything is meaningless"* (Ecclesiastes 1:2).

He says that wisdom is meaningless and pleasures are meaningless. He's had it all. There isn't anything he hasn't tried, and everything is useless, pointless, foolish, and empty apart from God. Through this book, Solomon warns us that often at the end of our lives we look back, and what we thought was so important just wasn't, and what we didn't think mattered, really did. He admitted that when he forgot God, he lost his way. It's hard to look back and see the "if onlys." He warns that God will bring every deed into judgment (even what we thought was a hidden thing). Solomon also teaches us in Ecclesiastes 3:1-8 that:

> *1 There is a time for everything,*
> *and a season for every activity under heaven:*
> *2 a time to be born and a time to die,*
> *a time to plant and a time to uproot,*
> *3 a time to kill and a time to heal,*
> *a time to tear down and a time to build,*
> *4 a time to weep and a time to laugh,*
> *a time to mourn and a time to dance,*
> *5 a time to scatter stones and a time to gather them,*
> *a time to embrace and a time to refrain,*
> *6 a time to search and a time to give up,*
> *a time to keep and a time to throw away,*
> *7 a time to tear and a time to mend,*
> *a time to be silent and a time to speak,*
> *8 a time to love and a time to hate,*
> *a time for war and a time for peace.*

Life without God is empty and hollow, and it will produce loneliness, bitterness, and hopelessness in your life. But with God, your life can have real meaning to the end when your eyes stay on Him and the eternal life that He promises with Him. Such profound advice from one who has been around the block a few times!

Before we end this chapter, let's take another look at the sins of Saul and David. Now, I know that sin is sin in the Lord's eyes. So what was the difference between Saul and David's responses to the Lord? David repented and Saul didn't, and THAT is what is important to the Lord. Another illustration of this can be found in the actions and reactions of Judas and Peter in the New Testament.

Matthew 26:23-25:

Jesus replied, "The one who has dipped his hand into the bowl with me will betray me. The Son of Man will go just as it is written about him. But woe to that man who betrays the Son of Man! It would be better for him if he had not been born."

Then Judas, the one who would betray him, said, "Surely not I, Rabbi?"

Jesus answered, "Yes, it is you."

Luke 22:47-48:

While he was still speaking a crowd came up, and the man who was called Judas, one of the Twelve, was leading them. He approached Jesus to kiss him, but Jesus asked him, "Judas, are you betraying the Son of Man with a kiss?"

Matthew 27:3-5:

When Judas, who had betrayed him, saw that Jesus was condemned, he was seized with remorse and returned the thirty silver coins to the chief priests and the elders. "I have sinned," he said, "for I have betrayed innocent blood."

"What is that to us?" they replied. "That's your responsibility."

So Judas threw the money into the temple and left. Then he went away and hanged himself.

John 17:12:

While I was with them, I protected them and kept them safe by that name you gave me. None has been lost except the one doomed to destruction so that Scripture would be fulfilled.

Luke 22:54-62:

Then seizing him, they led him away and took him into the house of the high priest. Peter followed at a distance. But when they had kindled a fire in the middle of the courtyard and had sat down together, Peter sat down with them. A servant girl saw him seated there in the firelight. She looked closely at him and said, "This man was with him."

But he denied it. "Woman, I don't know him," he said.

A little later someone else saw him and said, "You also are one of them."

"Man, I am not!" Peter replied.

About an hour later another asserted, "Certainly this fellow was with him, for he is a Galilean."

Peter replied, "Man, I don't know what you're talking about!" Just as he was speaking, the rooster crowed. The Lord turned and looked straight at Peter. Then Peter remembered the word the Lord had spoken to him: "Before the rooster crows today, you will disown me three times." And he went outside and wept bitterly.

John 21:14-17:

This was now the third time Jesus appeared to his disciples after he was raised from the dead.

*When they had finished eating, Jesus said
to Simon Peter, "Simon son of John, do you truly
love me more than these?"*

*"Yes, Lord," he said, "you know that I love
you."*

Jesus said, "Feed my lambs."

*Again Jesus said, "Simon son of John, do
you truly love me?"*

*He answered, "Yes, Lord, you know that I
love you."*

Jesus said, "Take care of my sheep."

*The third time he said to him, "Simon son
of John, do you love me?"*

*Peter was hurt because Jesus asked him the
third time, "Do you love me?" He said, "Lord, you
know all things; you know that I love you."*

Jesus said, "Feed my sheep...."

Luke 24:34:

*and saying, "It is true! The Lord has risen and has
appeared to Simon."*

Can you see it? There was no repentance from Judas, and he
was doomed to destruction. On the other hand, Peter's heartfelt
repentance resulted in a personal visit from the risen Jesus, and Peter
was thereafter used in a mighty way in building Christ's church.

If, by chance, you ever think that your sin is too great and the
Lord will never forgive you, let me just say, you are wrong. There is
only one sin that He will not forgive, and that is the sin of turning
your back on Jesus as your Savior by not listening to His Spirit
leading you to salvation. Other than that, He has promised to forgive
your EVERY sin that is confessed and then cleanse you from all your
unrighteousness. *If we confess our sins, he is faithful and just and
will forgive us our sins and purify us from all unrighteousness*
(I John 1:9).

But, there is one other flaw that must be addressed. When
God blesses us with gifts, they are to be used for Him. We are never

to be prideful or for any reason think that we had anything to do with them. God gives and equips all of His children with everything they need to serve Him on this earth. So let these kings be used to teach us, not only through their good times, but through their bad times as well.

CHAPTER 10

JESUS'   SIGNPOSTS

"Rejected King": ✟ Pg. 215

Whether Old or New Testament, note the rejection of the true King of kings—Jesus. We have not been nor are we now very bright! If you have not done so, choose Him <u>today</u> as your King, Lord, and Savior—you don't know when your last heartbeat will take place!

● ...John 18:37, *"You are a king, then!" said Pilate. Jesus answered, "You are right in saying I am a king. In fact, for this reason I was born, and for this I came into the world, to testify to the truth. Everyone on the side of truth listens to me."*

● ...John 19:14-19, *"Here is your king," Pilate said to the Jews. But they shouted, "Take him away! Take him away! Crucify him!" "Shall I crucify your king?" Pilate asked. "We have no king but Caesar," the chief priests answered. Finally Pilate handed him over to them to be crucified. So the soldiers took charge of Jesus. Carrying his own cross, he went out to the place of the Skull (which in Aramaic is called Golgotha). Here they crucified him, and with him two others--one on each side and Jesus in the middle. Pilate had a notice prepared and fastened to the cross. It read: JESUS OF NAZARETH, THE KING OF THE JEWS.*

"David, Bathsheba, & Solomon": ✝ Pg. 224

Truly God's GRACE in action: **G**od's **R**iches **A**t **C**hrist's **E**xpense!

- …Matthew 1:6, 16, *and Jesse the father of King David. David was the father of Solomon, whose mother had been Uriah's wife, …*

  16and Jacob the father of Joseph, the husband of Mary, of whom was born Jesus, who is called Christ.

Lesson 10: The First Three Kings of Israel
Selected Passages from I and II Samuel
and I Kings 1 - 11

1. In I Samuel 8:5, what do the elders of Israel ask for? What was their reasoning for making that request? How spiritually healthy was that reason, and what was Samuel's response?

2. Who was Israel's first king? (I Samuel 10:21.)

3. From I Samuel 13 and 15, what kind of king was he?

4. Who was David, and what kind of man was he? (I Samuel 16.)

5. What did Saul think of David? (I Sam. 16-19.)

6. How did David handle the fact that Saul was trying to kill him? (I Samuel 4.) Is revenge ever the answer? (Romans 12:19.)

7. What flaw, like Moses, do you see in David? (I Samuel 25.) Who was Abigail and how did God use her to keep David from destructive behavior?

8. How did David show his godly character in II Sam. 9?

9. What was David's root sin that manifested itself in adultery and murder? (II Samuel 11.) What is your behavior a reflection of?

10. Why couldn't David see his own sin? Who had to help him? (II Samuel 12.)

11.   Was David sincerely sorry? (Psalm 51.) However, what were the consequences? (II Samuel 12:14) What kind of testimony was David to his enemies? Why should you care about your testimony to your enemies?

12.   In I Kings 1:28-30, who would become the next king of Israel?

13.   In I Kings 3, what did Solomon ask for, and what did God give him?

14.   What was Solomon's downfall? (I Kings 11:1-4.) What were the inevitable consequences?

15.   David and Solomon were used by God in great ways, yet, why did both of them have such sad endings? What should these two men remind you of about human nature and how badly you need God?

11

The Divided Kingdom and the Prophets

After the death of Solomon, the Kingdom of Israel went from bad to worse. The northern tribes revolted, resulting in two separate kingdoms. The Kingdom of Israel never had a good king who led them in the direction of the Almighty God. The Kingdom of Judah did not have many, but they at least had some. Each kingdom experienced disastrous consequences because of their evil kings. God sent prophets during this horrible time to confront the kings and the kingdoms about their sin. God deals with sin. Sometimes it may appear slow, but He will deal with EVERY sin. There are many times in the Old Testament where you see how God deals with sin in powerful and harsh ways. It's called judgment. We are experiencing God's patience today in our world. There is sin on every corner, and it seems like the world is getting away with it. Oh, but it is not! He is just so full of love for mankind that He is giving them every chance possible.

> *The Lord is not slow in keeping his promise, as*
> *some understand slowness. He is patient with you,*
> *not wanting anyone to perish, but everyone to come*
> *to repentance* (II Peter 3:9).

We are told by the apostle John in the Book of Revelation that there WILL come a time when His patience will be over, His grace will be removed, and He will pour out His wrath. THAT day will be called Judgment Day. ✞ Jesus, who is the Judge, will rule on all sin. So, you see, your sin and mine will either be dealt with at the Cross of Christ or at the final Judgment when, I must bring to your attention, it will be too late for any redemption. That's why today is the day of salvation. No one knows when God's patience is going to run out; and then, for those who have not taken their sin seriously, they will see the side of God that isn't pretty but is Holy and Just.

For the Israelite kingdoms, the Lord sent prophets to get them to turn from their wickedness and return to their God. These very different men had the very same message—repent or be judged. These prophets are not all in chronological order in the Scriptures, and they are divided into two groups called the Major and Minor Prophets. They are called that because of the length of their book, NOT because of their importance. Here is a list of the prophets that the Lord sent to the two separate kingdoms:

MAJOR PROPHETS
        Isaiah
        Jeremiah
        Lamentations (written by Jeremiah)
        Ezekiel
        Daniel

MINOR PROPHETS
        Hosea
        Joel
        Amos
        Obadiah
        Jonah
        Micah
        Nahum
        Habakkuk
        Zephaniah
        Haggai
        Zachariah
        Malachi

I am not going to address every king or every prophet. I think that, for the most part, not many of the kings are too noteworthy. But you can at least see, again, how little the Lord had to work with; and yet He never gave up, because if He had we all would be lost and living a life that was meaningless and without hope. I can't even fathom that thought.

I do want to show you an example of the wickedness of the Kingdom of Israel. For this example, the reigning king was Ahab. His wife was Jezebel. In I Kings 16, it says that Ahab did more evil in the eyes of the Lord than any king before him. His pagan wife turned him to the god Baal, and he even set up an altar for Baal in the temple of the Lord. The chapter also says that he provoked the Lord more than any king before him. God sent to Ahab the prophet Elijah. To start with, the Lord had Elijah tell Ahab there would be no rain for the next few years except at his word—meaning a devastating famine would hit the kingdom. Then the Lord told Elijah to run and hide for awhile, and He would supply his needs. Three years later, Elijah came back and met with Ahab. Ahab called him a troublemaker. Of course, it's so much easier passing the buck and blaming the messenger than looking at the facts of his own disobedience and thereafter reaping the consequences.

Elijah's strength in the Lord enabled him to have no fear of Ahab and to be confident in his God. In fact, he made a challenge to the king. In I Kings 18:19-40, read this incredible story of God's power and one man's belief. He stood alone with his God, and dared the prophets of Baal and Asherah to a duel:

> *19Now summon the people from all over Israel to meet me on Mount Carmel. And bring the four hundred and fifty prophets of Baal and the four hundred prophets of Asherah, who eat at Jezebel's table."*
>
> *20So Ahab sent word throughout all Israel and assembled the prophets on Mount Carmel. 21Elijah went before the people and said, "How long will you waver between two opinions? If the LORD is God, follow him; but if Baal is God, follow him."*
>
> *But the people said nothing.*
>
> *22Then Elijah said to them, "I am the only one of the LORD's prophets left, but Baal has four hundred and fifty prophets. 23Get two bulls for us.*

*Let them choose one for themselves, and let them
cut it into pieces and put it on the wood but not set
fire to it. I will prepare the other bull and put it on
the wood but not set fire to it. 24Then you call on
the name of your god, and I will call on the name of
the LORD. The god who answers by fire—he is
God."*

*Then all the people said, "What you say is
good."*

*25Elijah said to the prophets of Baal,
"Choose one of the bulls and prepare it first, since
there are so many of you. Call on the name of your
god, but do not light the fire." 26So they took the
bull given them and prepared it.*

*Then they called on the name of Baal from
morning till noon. "O Baal, answer us!" they
shouted. But there was no response; no one
answered. And they danced around the altar they
had made.*

*27At noon Elijah began to taunt them.
"Shout louder!" he said. "Surely he is a god!
Perhaps he is deep in thought, or busy, or traveling.
Maybe he is sleeping and must be awakened." 28So
they shouted louder and slashed themselves with
swords and spears, as was their custom, until their
blood flowed. 29Midday passed, and they continued
their frantic prophesying until the time for the
evening sacrifice. But there was no response, no
one answered, no one paid attention.*

*30Then Elijah said to all the people, "Come
here to me." They came to him, and he repaired the
altar of the LORD, which was in ruins. 31Elijah
took twelve stones, one for each of the tribes
descended from Jacob, to whom the word of the
LORD had come, saying, "Your name shall be
Israel." 32With the stones he built an altar in the
name of the LORD, and he dug a trench around it*

large enough to hold two seahs of seed. 33He arranged the wood, cut the bull into pieces and laid it on the wood. Then he said to them, "Fill four large jars with water and pour it on the offering and on the wood."

34"Do it again," he said, and they did it again.

"Do it a third time," he ordered, and they did it the third time. 35The water ran down around the altar and even filled the trench.

36At the time of sacrifice, the prophet Elijah stepped forward and prayed: "O LORD, God of Abraham, Isaac and Israel, let it be known today that you are God in Israel and that I am your servant and have done all these things at your command. 37Answer me, O LORD, answer me, so these people will know that you, O LORD, are God, and that you are turning their hearts back again."

38Then the fire of the LORD fell and burned up the sacrifice, the wood, the stones and the soil, and also licked up the water in the trench.

39When all the people saw this, they fell prostrate and cried, "The LORD—he is God! The LORD—he is God!"

40Then Elijah commanded them, "Seize the prophets of Baal. Don't let anyone get away!" They seized them, and Elijah had them brought down to the Kishon Valley and slaughtered there.

The Lord, He is God! That's the most powerful statement there is. It is the most truthful statement that ever was made about all the gods mankind worshiped down through the ages. What a sight that must have been to watch. Wouldn't you have loved to have been there?

The second miracle the Lord used Elijah for was to tell the king that rain was coming! At the time, there was not a cloud in the sky. Again, it demonstrated the power of real, solid faith. He knew his God. Read on in verses 41-46:

> *And Elijah said to Ahab, "Go, eat and drink, for there is the sound of a heavy rain." So Ahab went off to eat and drink, but Elijah climbed to the top of Carmel, bent down to the ground and put his face between his knees.*
>
> *"Go and look toward the sea," he told his servant. And he went up and looked.*
>
> *"There is nothing there," he said.*
>
> *Seven times Elijah said, "Go back."*
>
> *The seventh time the servant reported, "A cloud as small as a man's hand is rising from the sea."*
>
> *So Elijah said, "Go and tell Ahab, `Hitch up your chariot and go down before the rain stops you.'"*
>
> *Meanwhile, the sky grew black with clouds, the wind rose, a heavy rain came on and Ahab rode off to Jezreel. The power of the LORD came upon Elijah and, tucking his cloak into his belt, he ran ahead of Ahab all the way to Jezreel.*

Did you notice the third miracle in this same chapter? Elijah was able to outrun whatever Ahab rode off in. It wasn't Elijah's outstanding athletic ability; it was the power of God. I would dare say that Elijah had a very big day. He was on quite the spiritual high. I make mention of that because as good as spiritual highs are, they can be dangerous. One has to be very careful when one is experiencing them. Satan is just waiting in the wings to, with one move, slam you to the ground. I heard once that we are never closer to defeat than in our moments of greatest victory.

Elijah experienced three unexplainable events—miracles of God—in one day. Ahab went home and told his wife Jezebel all about the day's events. That woman was a real piece of work, and Satan was leading her. She had made it one of her missions to kill all the prophets of God. So when she heard all of this, she said regarding Elijah, *"May the gods deal with me, be it ever so severely, if by this time tomorrow I do not make your life like that of one of them"* (I Kings 19:2b).

Elijah got the message loud and clear and turned to mush. This powerful man of God took his spiritual eyes off his God, thus losing his power, and he became afraid. He ran for his life. This time he ran out of human fear, not because the Lord told him to. There is a big difference. He went about a day's journey into the desert, and then he sat down under a tree and prayed that he might die. He told the Lord to just take his life. One can understand his exhaustion from the day before, the news of Jezebel, and now the hike into the desert. This man was beat. When we are overtired, it is so easy to fall prey to self-pity. We really start feeling sorry for ourselves, and out it comes—a bunch of sobbing and whining. The Lord sent an angel to minister to him and give him food and drink to rebuild his physical strength. Elijah traveled for forty days and forty nights, and when he reached Horeb, the mountain of God, he went into a cave to spend the night. Apparently, this was not where the Lord wanted him. He might have been physically strengthened, but he still chose to stay in his snit of self-pity. Let me give you a little advice about staying in your "snit." You WILL miss the good that God has right in front of you. You can't see it because all you can see is YOU. You've got to read how this played out in I Kings 19:9-18:

> *9There he went into a cave and spent the night.*
>
> *And the word of the LORD came to him: "What are you doing here, Elijah?"*
>
> *10He replied, "I have been very zealous for the LORD God Almighty. The Israelites have rejected your covenant, broken down your altars, and put your prophets to death with the sword. I am the only one left, and now they are trying to kill me too."*
>
> *11The LORD said, "Go out and stand on the mountain in the presence of the LORD, for the LORD is about to pass by."*

Then a great and powerful wind tore the mountains apart and shattered the rocks before the LORD, but the LORD was not in the wind. After the wind there was an earthquake, but the LORD was not in the earthquake. 12After the earthquake came a fire, but the LORD was not in the fire. And after the fire came a gentle whisper. 13When Elijah heard it, he pulled his cloak over his face and went out and stood at the mouth of the cave.

Then a voice said to him, "What are you doing here, Elijah?"

14He replied, "I have been very zealous for the LORD God Almighty. The Israelites have rejected your covenant, broken down your altars, and put your prophets to death with the sword. I am the only one left, and now they are trying to kill me too."

15The LORD said to him, "Go back the way you came, and go to the Desert of Damascus. When you get there, anoint Hazael king over Aram. 16Also, anoint Jehu son of Nimshi king over Israel, and anoint Elisha son of Shaphat from Abel Meholah to succeed you as prophet. 17Jehu will put to death any who escape the sword of Hazael, and Elisha will put to death any who escape the sword of Jehu. 18Yet I reserve seven thousand in Israel— all whose knees have not bowed down to Baal and all whose mouths have not kissed him."

The Lord was going to minister to Elijah personally. Like all of us, Elijah expected to meet God in an over-the-top experience. He thought God would be in the wind, or the earthquake, or the fire; but instead, God met with him in a gentle whisper. God meets us in our quiet moments, or moments we least expect. We have to have our spiritual ears open to hear His voice—to sense His renewing power. We have to want it or we will miss it, and then miss God's blessing. Elijah did not want to hear God's voice. He pulled his coat over his ears and his face. The Lord asked him what he was still doing in that same emotional state. He wouldn't have been in that funk if he had chosen to hear God's sweet Voice of love and encouragement. But instead, he started that same old song and dance again. Look at verses 10 and 14. They are practically the same words. He gained nothing from the Lord's ministering to him because he chose not to. So then, all that comes out again are the same words of self-pity and defeat. This time, the Lord just simply TOLD him to go back the way he came and to go back to work and do the job He had called him to do. Get to work and you won't be able to think about yourself. No sympathy, because what can be accomplished sitting there and stewing in our own self-pity? Nothing! And we miss allowing the Lord to lift us back up to the abundant life He has given us. It's our call—our choice of attitude for any given situation.

Just in case you want to know what happened to Jezebel, she got exactly what the Lord said she would get.

> *"Throw her down!" Jehu said. So they threw her down, and some of her blood spattered the wall and the horses as they trampled her underfoot.*
> *Jehu went in and ate and drank. "Take care of that cursed woman," he said, "and bury her, for she was a king's daughter." But when they went out to bury her, they found nothing except her skull, her feet and her hands. They went back and told Jehu, who said, "This is the word of the LORD that he spoke through his servant Elijah the Tishbite: On the plot of ground at Jezreel dogs will devour Jezebel's flesh. Jezebel's body will be like refuse on the ground in the plot at Jezreel, so that no one will be able to say, `This is Jezebel'"* (2 Kings 9:33-37).

Jezebel knew better. She was warned. God's patience ran out and she faced His judgment, just like He said would happen to her, and to all who will not do what He says.

Because of their rebellious and evil lifestyle, in 722 B.C., the Kingdom of Israel fell to the Assyrians, never to become again what it once was.

One of the prophets sent to the Kingdom of Judah was Isaiah. Even the prophets had to be prepared for the work God called them to do. Being a prophet was far from an easy job, and it was a very unappreciated and thankless job. One had to be called by God, or there wouldn't have been any volunteers, for sure. But once called, as He promises, God prepared and provided. God gave Isaiah a personal experience that, I dare say, he never forgot, even in the most difficult times. Picture this in Isaiah 6:1-8:

> In the year that King Uzziah died, I saw the Lord seated on a throne, high and exalted, and the train of his robe filled the temple. Above him were seraphs, each with six wings: With two wings they covered their faces, with two they covered their feet, and with two they were flying. And they were calling to one another:
> "Holy, holy, holy is the LORD Almighty; the whole earth is full of his glory." At the sound of their voices the doorposts and thresholds shook and the temple was filled with smoke.
> "Woe to me!" I cried. "I am ruined! For I am a man of unclean lips, and I live among a people of unclean lips, and my eyes have seen the King, the LORD Almighty."
> Then one of the seraphs flew to me with a live coal in his hand, which he had taken with tongs from the altar. With it he touched my mouth and said, "See, this has touched your lips; your guilt is taken away and your sin atoned for."
> Then I heard the voice of the Lord saying, "Whom shall I send? And who will go for us?"
> And I said, "Here am I. Send me!"

Did you notice the order of his experience? First, he saw the Lord in all of His glory and holiness. Secondly, he then couldn't help but see who he really was without the Lord and the Lord's willingness to change him. Finally, when the Lord asked who He should send to share this message the people needed to hear, he was the first to volunteer! It was like this was his chance to say thank you for all the Lord had done for him. I know the Lord would love to hear all of us say thank you to Him with our words, yes, but most of all through our lives in service for Him. It's the least we can do. And with that kind of love and gratitude, Isaiah stepped out to do his job, and what a job God did through him! Hundreds of years before Jesus was even born, look what the Lord gave Isaiah to prophesy:

Isaiah 7:14:

Therefore the Lord himself will give you a sign: The virgin will be with child and will give birth to a son, and will call him Immanuel.

Isaiah 9:6-7:

For to us a child is born,
  to us a son is given,
  and the government will be on his
  shoulders. ✞
And he will be called
  Wonderful Counselor, Mighty God,
  Everlasting Father, Prince of Peace.
Of the increase of his government and peace
  there will be no end.
He will reign on David's throne
  and over his kingdom,
establishing and upholding it
  with justice and righteousness
  from that time on and forever.
The zeal of the LORD Almighty
  will accomplish this.

Isaiah 35:4-6:

say to those with fearful hearts,
  "Be strong, do not fear;
  your God will come,

he will come with vengeance;
with divine retribution
he will come to save you."
Then will the eyes of the blind be opened
and the ears of the deaf unstopped.
Then will the lame leap like a deer,
and the mute tongue shout for joy.
Water will gush forth in the wilderness
and streams in the desert.

Isaiah 40:1-5, 9:

Comfort, comfort my people,
says your God.
Speak tenderly to Jerusalem,
and proclaim to her
that her hard service has been completed,
that her sin has been paid for,
that she has received from the LORD's hand
double for all her sins.
A voice of one calling:
"In the desert prepare
the way for the LORD;
make straight in the wilderness
a highway for our God.
Every valley shall be raised up,
every mountain and hill made low;
the rough ground shall become level,
the rugged places a plain.
And the glory of the LORD will be revealed,
and all mankind together will see it.
For the mouth of the LORD has spoken."

You who bring good tidings to Zion,
go up on a high mountain.
You who bring good tidings to Jerusalem,
lift up your voice with a shout,
lift it up, do not be afraid;

say to the towns of Judah,
"Here is your God!"

Isaiah 49:6:

he says:
 "It is too small a thing for you to be my servant
  to restore the tribes of Jacob
  and bring back those of Israel I have kept.
 I will also make you a light for the Gentiles,
  that you may bring my salvation to the
  ends of the earth."

Isaiah 50:6:

I offered my back to those who beat me,
  my cheeks to those who pulled out my beard;
 I did not hide my face
  from mocking and spitting.

Isaiah. 53:1-7, 9, 12:

Who has believed our message,
  and to whom has the arm of the LORD been
  revealed?
He grew up before him like a tender shoot,
  and like a root out of dry ground.
 He had no beauty or majesty to attract us to him,
  nothing in his appearance that we
  should desire him.
He was despised and rejected by men,
  a man of sorrows, and familiar with
  suffering.
 Like one from whom men hide their faces
  he was despised, and we esteemed him not.
Surely he took up our infirmities
  and carried our sorrows,
  yet we considered him stricken by God,

smitten by him, and afflicted.
But he was pierced for our transgressions,
he was crushed for our iniquities;
the punishment that brought us peace was upon him,
and by his wounds we are healed.
We all, like sheep, have gone astray,
each of us has turned to his own way;
and the LORD has laid on him
the iniquity of us all.
He was oppressed and afflicted,
yet he did not open his mouth;
he was led like a lamb to the slaughter,
and as a sheep before her shearers is silent,
so he did not open his mouth.

He was assigned a grave with the wicked,
and with the rich in his death,
though he had done no violence,
nor was any deceit in his mouth.

Therefore I will give him a portion among the great,
and he will divide the spoils with the strong,
because he poured out his life unto death,
and was numbered with the transgressors.
For he bore the sin of many,
and made intercession for the transgressors.

Another prophet named Jeremiah, under the Lord's leading, prophesied that the Kingdom of Judah would be taken into captivity by the Babylonians. He warned them that this was going to happen. He lamented over them as he wrote the book of Lamentations 1–2. He could hardly stand it. In chapter 3:19-25, he tried to give them some hope.

I remember my affliction and my wandering,
the bitterness and the gall.
I well remember them,
and my soul is downcast within me.

Yet this I call to mind
and therefore I have hope:
Because of the LORD's great love we are not
consumed,
for his compassions never fail.
They are new every morning;
great is your faithfulness.
I say to myself, "The LORD is my portion;
therefore I will wait for him."
The LORD is good to those whose hope is in him,
to the one who seeks him;

The kingdom had forsaken the Lord time after time, and in 586 B.C., Jerusalem was destroyed and the kingdom was taken captive. Sad, sad, day! And to think that the story could have been so much different if they would have just obeyed and not rebelled against God! Are we hearing God's warnings to us? I pray that we are, because as every prophecy was or will be fulfilled to the letter in the Old Testament, every prophecy WILL also be fulfilled in the New. Consider yourself warned.

When reading the prophets' books and hearing their prophecies, I was so taken by their willingness to tap into God's wisdom and understanding. God will give us what we need, especially when we feel "unequipped" for the task. He did that with the prophet Ezekiel. He admitted strongly in chapter two that he was called of God, who had specific instructions for him. He said the Lord was sending him to a rebellious nation. In other words, it wasn't going to be easy. He said God wanted him to spare no words whether they listened or not, because the Lord always wanted His people to look back and see that there had been a prophet among them. He said the Lord was extremely hurt by what His people were doing. Go after their heart. Pull at their emotions—anything to get their attention.

I remember that when my husband and I were raising our boys, our methods of getting THEIR attention, when necessary, had to be completely different for each boy. With one son, all I had to do when he would not respond to my instructions was get the spoon out of the drawer and he came a runnin'. With the other one, I really think I could have beat him with that spoon (which I NEVER would have done), and he wouldn't have budged or buckled. But if I said that he hurt my feelings or disappointed me, oh my, the crocodile tears would fall. So I think the Lord was using various avenues to get His people to sit up and take notice. Ezekiel was a younger contemporary of Jeremiah. While Jeremiah ministered to the people still in Judah, Ezekiel prophesied during the time when the Kingdom of Judah walked into captivity. He took them by the hand in that difficult time, walked side by side with them, yet did not mince words in prophesying the truth. God provided the words needed for Ezekiel to tell the future, some of which has since been fulfilled, but also the future that has yet to be fulfilled. In Ezekiel 1:4b-6 &10, God gave Ezekiel a vision. In this vision, he saw a fire.

> *The center of the fire looked like glowing metal, and in the fire was what looked like four living creatures. In appearance their form was that of a man, but each of them had four faces and four wings.*

> *Their faces looked like this: Each of the four had the face of a man, and on the right side each had the face of a lion, and on the left the face of an ox; each also had the face of an eagle.*

Where have I heard that before? That's right! In Revelation! The apostle John saw a similar vision in Revelation 4:6b-7:

> *In the center, around the throne, were four living creatures, and they were covered with eyes, in front and in back. The first living creature was like a lion, the second was like an ox, the third had a face like a man, the fourth was like a flying eagle.*

Ezekiel was prophesying a Savior, and he didn't even realize it. John was describing the character of Christ Himself. The lion symbolizes the King of kings. The ox symbolizes Christ as the faithful, hardworking servant. The face of a man symbolizes Christ's humanity—the Son of Man—living on this earth to accomplish His mission at the Cross. The eagle symbolizes His deity. He soars with power because He is the Son of God. Each of the four Gospels takes one of those characteristics and demonstrates it: Matthew explains how He is the King. Mark shows Jesus as the faithful Servant. Dr. Luke describes His humanity. John really centers in on Jesus, the Son of God! So from Ezekiel to Revelation, we are able to see Jesus. Ezekiel was prophesying the coming of a Savior. But he also was prophesying, like John, the second coming of Christ, when He returns to claim back the title of this earth to make all things right again and to banish evil and the evil one to eternal hell. What a future we have, brothers and sisters in Christ! Our battle has already been won, so just hang on! Take heart! God's kingdom will never be destroyed. If you are upset by threats of war and evil leaders, remember that GOD, not world leaders, decides the outcome of history. Under God's protection, God's kingdom is indestructible. If you belong to God's kingdom, you are secure forevermore!

There is one more prophet that I would like to bring up, because he showed just how far the Lord would go to get His chosen people to understand His love for them. He called Hosea to demonstrate this through his own life. God told the prophet Hosea to find a wife, and told him ahead of time that she would be unfaithful to him. Although she would bear many children, some of these offspring would be fathered by others. In obedience to God, Hosea married Gomer. His relationship with her, her adultery, and their children became living, prophetic examples to Israel. It is a love story—real, tragic, and true. Taking it higher than the story of a young man and wife, it tells of God's love for His people and their response. A covenant had been made, and God had been faithful. But Israel, like Gomer, was adulterous and unfaithful, turning from God's love and giving her allegiance to false gods. Then, after warning of judgment, God reaffirmed His love and offered reconciliation. His love and mercy were overflowing, but justice would be served. Hosea willingly submitted to His Lord's direction and request. He experienced great hurt over the unfaithfulness of his wife, just as God did with the unfaithfulness of His people.

When Gomer left with no plans to return, even after all she had done to him, Hosea went to rescue her. He found her and brought her home again, fully forgiven. Like Israel, like you and me, sin separated us from God, leaving us with no chance of ever being able to get back to Him on our own. Not one of us could ever save ourselves, so God comes after us to redeem us, and He rebuilds the broken bridge of our relationship with Him using His own Son. The prophet Hosea was willing to give his life for the cause. Jesus was willing to give His life for the cause. Are we willing to give our lives for the cause (of Christ, of course)?

In the middle of all of this negativity and darkness, in captivity, there were a couple of stories that were full of light and hope and so very positive. One of them was the story of Shadrach, Meshach, and Abednego. These three men were noticed by their captors and were considered to be of great value to the Babylonians; however, they would not bow down to the ninety-foot gold image of King Nebuchadnezzar and worship it. These three Israelites, even though in captivity, would not succumb to the Babylonian pressure found all around them. That's amazing! When asked why they wouldn't bow down, and what god was going to rescue them from their punishment in the fiery furnace, their reply was given in Daniel 3:16-23:

> *Shadrach, Meshach and Abednego replied to the king, "O Nebuchadnezzar, we do not need to defend ourselves before you in this matter. If we are thrown into the blazing furnace, the God we serve is able to save us from it, and he will rescue us from your hand, O king. But even if he does not, we want you to know, O king, that we will not serve your gods or worship the image of gold you have set up."*

> *Then Nebuchadnezzar was furious with Shadrach, Meshach and Abednego, and his attitude toward them changed. He ordered the furnace heated seven times hotter than usual and commanded some of the strongest soldiers in his army to tie up Shadrach, Meshach and Abednego and throw them into the blazing furnace. So these men, wearing their robes, trousers, turbans and*

other clothes, were bound and thrown into the blazing furnace. The king's command was so urgent and the furnace so hot that the flames of the fire killed the soldiers who took up Shadrach, Meshach and Abednego, and these three men, firmly tied, fell into the blazing furnace.

What a story! King Nebuchadnezzar stood at the door of the furnace expecting to see them fry; but instead he kept counting the figures inside, and he came up with four, knowing that only three were put in there. He called the men out, and only three came out; but it was very clear that this was the beginning of the king's turnaround. Not only had he seen an angel of the Lord protecting the three men, he saw that these men were not even scorched. They didn't even smell like smoke.

King Nebuchadnezzar had another close encounter with the Lord God, and that was through a very unusual dream, which came true. The king was actually driven away from the people and reduced to eating grass like cattle. His hair grew like the feathers of an eagle and his nails like the claws of a bird. Finally, after the appointed time had passed, the king raised his eyes toward heaven, and his sanity was restored. He then praised the Most High. He honored and glorified the Lord! God restored Nebuchadnezzar's honor, splendor, and his kingdom. The king learned two valuable lessons through all of this; not only that God is God and there is none other, but also that whoever walks in pride the Lord will humble. We would like to think that he became a member of the family of God, but only God sees the heart of man.

Another devoted man of God, who lived during the kingdom of Judah's captivity under King Nebuchadnezzar, King Belshazzar, and King Darius, was Daniel. He, too, was recognized by the Babylonians for all his God-given gifts, abilities, and wisdom; and he was raised to a very important position. As a foreigner, this made the other administrators of Babylonia jealous. Daniel was given positions they should have gotten. They wanted him out of the way, but Daniel was not corrupt or negligent, and was so trustworthy that they couldn't find a way to bring him down. What a compliment! The way we live our lives on a consistent basis, in the privacy of our homes and when we are out in public, determines the way people describe us. The one other noticeable quality Daniel had, that I pray is the most noticed, is that he lived, worshiped, talked about, and prayed to his God. It was that close and committed relationship with God that made him the terrific kid he was; and yet that is what they used to try to get rid of Daniel. The administrators got the king to sign a decree that for the next thirty days, all prayers were to be prayed to King Darius, and him alone. Without thinking, because he and Daniel had a very good relationship, the king's pride got in the way, and he signed the decree. Sure enough, there was no way Daniel was going to pray to anyone else other than his God. He didn't even shut the curtains to try to hide what he was doing. He was not ashamed of his God. When the administrators brought this to the attention of the king, he was sick! But the decree had been signed, and into the den of lions Daniel was thrown! The king couldn't sleep that night, and at the first light of dawn he got up and hurried to the lion's den. He called out to Daniel, and with no hesitation Daniel told the king that his God had sent His angel to shut the mouths of the lions. These are not fairy tales. These are true stories that help us see who God really is and what He expects from us, and that He will ALWAYS be there with us through it ALL!

I have often wondered when I read stories like these two, or of martyrs of the faith: would I be willing to face my death or go to my death for the sake of Christ? Could I make that confident stand, whatever the cost? I would dare say that you have asked that of yourself as well. With all confidence, I KNOW we would IF we knew our God as well as they did. That's the key—KNOWING your God so well. I believe there wouldn't even be a hesitation. That's why getting to know Him better should be a goal we strive for every day—a priority. We don't know when we might be called to make a very important stand for the Savior who gave His all for you and me.

CHAPTER 11

JESUS'   SIGNPOSTS

"Judgment Day": ✞ Pg. 237

● ...Philippians 2:9-11, *Therefore God exalted him* [Jesus] *to the highest place and gave him the name that is above every name, that at the name of Jesus every knee should bow, in heaven and on earth and under the earth, and every tongue confess that Jesus Christ is Lord, to the glory of God the Father.*

● ...John 5:22-27, *Moreover, the Father judges no one, but has entrusted all judgment to the Son* [Jesus], *that all may honor the Son just as they honor the Father. He who does not honor the Son does not honor the Father, who sent him. "I tell you the truth, whoever hears my word and believes him who sent me has eternal life and will not be condemned; he has crossed over from death to life. I tell you the truth, a time is coming and has now come when the dead will hear the voice of the Son of God and those who hear will live. For as the Father has life in himself, so he has granted the Son to have life in himself. And he has given him authority to judge because he is the Son of Man.*

- ...2 Peter 3:7, *By the same word the present heavens and earth are reserved for fire, being kept for the day of judgment and destruction of ungodly men.*

- ...Romans 2:5, *But because of your stubbornness and your unrepentant heart, you are storing up wrath against yourself for the day of God's wrath, when his righteous judgment will be revealed.*

- ...Matthew 11:24, *But I tell you that it will be more bearable for Sodom on the day of judgment than for you."*

"Child is Born": ✟ Pg. 247

- ...Matthew 1:18-21, *This is how the birth of Jesus Christ came about: His mother Mary was pledged to be married to Joseph, but before they came together, she was found to be with child through the Holy Spirit. Because Joseph her husband was a righteous man and did not want to expose her to public disgrace, he had in mind to divorce her quietly. But after he had considered this, an angel of the Lord appeared to him in a dream and said, "Joseph son of David, do not be afraid to take Mary home as your wife, because what is conceived in her is from the Holy Spirit. She will give birth to a son, and you are to give him the name Jesus, because he will save his people from their sins."*

Lesson 11:
The Divided Kingdom and the Prophets
Selected Passages from the Kings and the Prophets

1.   What happened to the kingdom of Israel after Solomon's death? What seemed to be their severest weakness?

2.   Time and time again, Israel rejected God and His commands. Same holds true for today. What does 2 Peter 3:9 say about why God is patient?   When will His patience run out? (Revelation 20: 11-15.)

3.   What was the job and message of a prophet? Was the job an easy or pleasant one? What, then, motivated each prophet to persist?

4.   Who was King Ahab, and who was he married to? (I Kings 16: 29-33.)

5.   Who was Elijah? What message did he bring to Ahab? (I Kings 17: 1-6.)

6.   Describe the scene at Mount Carmel in I Kings 18:16-40.

7.   What two other miracles did Elijah experience in I Kings 18:41-46?

8.   Even after all the miracles in chapter 18, what happened to Elijah in I Kings 19? What extensive damage can self-pity do?

9.   What eventually happened to the kingdom of Israel and the kingdom of Judah?

10.   The kingdom of Israel never returned from captivity, but what did the prophet Jeremiah promise the kingdom of Judah in Jeremiah 29:10-14?

11.   Compare Ezekiel 1:4-14 with Revelation 4:6-7. Who were they both describing?

12.   What does the prophet Isaiah say of the coming Messiah— Jesus the Savior?

13.   How did the prophet Hosea's wife and the marriage God called him to, compare to the actions of God's chosen people?

14.   In Daniel 3 and 6, what were these four men willing to do? How can you KNOW that you would do the same?

12

The End of Captivity, Queen Esther, and God's Providence

After their captivity in Babylonia, the Israelites of the kingdom of Judah returned to their homeland, the Promised Land. The first two groups to go back were led by Shesbazzar and Zerubbabel. The third group was led back by the prophet Ezra. This prophet knew God's Word and obeyed it. He was filled with God's wisdom, and above all, He loved his Lord. He definitely was the right man for this exciting event. Yes, these Jews were going back to the Promised Land, but it lay in ruins. When they were captured, the Babylonians destroyed everything. They tore down the walls and destroyed the city of Jerusalem and God's temple. So these people had their work cut out for them. They knew the challenges ahead, but it was their land and God's city, and they were finally FREE.

The rebuilding was going to be a long, hard process. It was all that, and eventually discouragement set in. So God sent the prophets Haggai, Zechariah, and Malachi to encourage them to continue. The prophet Nehemiah was used by God to rebuild the walls of Jerusalem and help renew their faith. These prophets were like spiritual cheerleaders to help them keep going! When we are faced with a mountain before us, and it feels like it's more than we can handle, or that we bit off more than we could chew, it seems God sends just the right person or experience to show Himself through them, and we realize we need to let go and let God. We are able to pick ourselves back up and feel the reenergizing sensation to take the next step forward, and that is always the right direction.

As I mentioned to you in our study of Ruth in Chapter 9 about my change of perspective about her story, I also have taken a different perspective about Esther's story than my previously held traditional view. Let's take a look and see what you think.

Esther's story began 103 years after Nebuchadnezzar had taken the Jews into captivity. Esther's parents must have been among those exiles who CHOSE not to return to Jerusalem, even though they should have. Remember, it was Jeremiah who prophesied and warned the Israelites from the kingdom of Judah that they would go into captivity, but he also said these words in Jeremiah 29:10-14:

> *This is what the LORD says: "When seventy years are completed for Babylon, I will come to you and fulfill my gracious promise to bring you back to this place. For I know the plans I have for you," declares the LORD, "plans to prosper you and not to harm you, plans to give you hope and a future. Then you will call upon me and come and pray to me, and I will listen to you. You will seek me and find me when you seek me with all your heart. I will be found by you," declares the LORD, "and will bring you back from captivity. I will gather you from all the nations and places where I have banished you," declares the LORD, "and will bring you back to the place from which I carried you into exile."*

That sounds pretty clear to me. God expected His people to return to the Promised Land ✞ and rebuild it and His temple. But only 50,000 returned. The rest, like the American Dream, bought into the Persian Dream of prosperity, success, personal safety, and comfort—and that can damage, if not kill, one's true faith in God.

The Jewish exiles had great freedom in Persia, Babylonia, and more stayed in Persia than returned to the Promised Land. I can about guess why. For many, their faith in the Lord had dwindled. They were so discouraged and depressed about their captivity that they turned away from the Lord and became intertwined with the pagans. Their faith was so small that they didn't have much to demonstrate to their children. So when the prophets said that it was time to go "home," they were not interested. Why would they want to go back to ruins and have to work their poor little fingers to the bone, when they could just as well stay put and enjoy the ease and luxury of Persia? I believe so strongly that they were out of God's will—not out of His care—but out of His will.

For many, many years as I read and heard the story of Esther, I made her such a heroine. In fact, like so many figures in the Bible, we have a way of making them the center of attention and glory, when it was the Lord working His plan all along, and then He doesn't seem to get any credit. As humans, we seem to want to see our heroes and almost feel a part of their glory and honor, because they are people just like us. I knew that the Lord's name was never mentioned in this book, but I was led to believe it was because the Lord wanted us to see His presence even when His name wasn't mentioned. To some extent, that is true. The Lord does show His grace and His plan when His name isn't mentioned, not BECAUSE of Esther and Mordecai, but IN SPITE of them. I know that might sound harsh, but according to Jeremiah, Esther's family should have been back at the old homestead. Oh, I know that Mordecai does not bow down to Haman when we get into the story. One can have convictions from way back, but that doesn't mean one is fully committed to God. Mordecai does not express WHY he does not bow down. It's like in his heart, he knew better. His conscience wouldn't let him. As we go through the story, let me point out places where God's name should have been shouted from the rooftops, but wasn't. In the book of Song of Solomon, God's name is not mentioned either, but every masculine pronoun refers to Him, with maybe one exception. But in the book of Esther, not only is His name not mentioned; there is no pronoun referring to Him. However, the pagan king's name is mentioned 192 times. What does that tell you?

The book of Esther really shows the providence of God, meaning "God providing." God is at the steering wheel of the universe—shifting and directing His plan into motion, even when people do not want to be led. This book shows how God is behind the scenes, shifting and directing His wayward people. They would have been slain otherwise. If that isn't real love, I don't know what is; and yet His name is not mentioned. But I also know that *All Scripture is God-breathed...* ✝ (II Timothy 3:16a). So for His reasons alone, God chose to not have His name mentioned in this book. And as we all know, He knows best. Deuteronomy 31:18

might give a clue to why God's name is not mentioned in the book of Esther, and it's because His face was hidden, *"And I will certainly hide my face on that day because of all their wickedness in turning to other gods."*

When one does not know Him, see Him, feel Him, love Him, or experience Him, one will never mention Him; and yet He still loves us and will accomplish His plan, even when He doesn't have much to work with.

As the story begins, you get a taste of the kind of environment this nation had. A nation follows its leader, and the leader was King Xerxes. He was powerful—he was in charge of 127 provinces, and he reigned in the citadel (palace) of Susa. In the third year of his reign, he gave a banquet for all of his nobles and officials. For 180 days he displayed the vast wealth of his kingdom and the splendor and glory of his majesty. What a blowhard, full of ego, self-consumed, and selfish. He allowed everyone who came to have as much to drink as they wished. At the same time, Queen Vashti was having a banquet of her own for the women in the royal palace.

On the seventh day, when the king was in "high spirits" (drunk), he commanded his servants to bring Queen Vashti, wearing her royal crown, to display her beauty to the people and nobles because she was a gorgeous woman. But when she got the message, she refused to come! A queen never refused the king, but she did. Did you ever wonder how she had the courage to do that at this particular time? I put myself in her shoes. Remember, she had been at this women's banquet, and there is no doubt in my mind that these women had been discussing their men. They probably all concurred that they were treated with no respect and love, just used when called upon. I think they joined together and said, "NO MORE." She was hoppin' mad and knew that the consequences would be severe; but for all women, I believe she made a stand. We never hear from her again in Scripture, other than that she was dismissed as queen, but she was one brave gal.

The king burned with anger at the queen's refusal to obey him. He got his seven nobles around him, and they had to decide what to do. These nobles were not too concerned about Queen Vashti, but rather about their "little women" who were at the same banquet. They turned into nervous Nellies, fearful that there would be no end of the women's disrespect and discord. They were afraid they would lose control of their women. So it was agreed that Vashti would never enter the presence of the king again, and her royal position would be given to someone else who would "act" properly. They made sure that a memo went out to every province, all 127 of them, proclaiming in each province's individual dialect so there would be no misunderstanding, that every man should be ruler over his own household.

Chapter two starts with the word "later." Later, when the king's anger subsided, could mean when he became sober, or it could have been a bigger span in time. According to history, King Xerxes had gone to war against a nation and lost. War at that time wasn't to protect from an enemy, it was to acquire more and more—a never ending desire for material things and power. It was humiliating to have to come home with his tail tucked between his legs, dragging his defeat behind him. When he got home, there was no queen to console him. He must have gone into such a depressed funk that his attendants knew they better figure out something, and fast. They decided to put out a search for a new queen. Memos went out to every province that the king was going to appoint commissioners to go into every province and bring all the beautiful girls into the harem at the palace. That could have been one time when the girls cast aside or teased for their homely looks were silently cheering. Esther was chosen because she was very beautiful. Now, I do feel for her because she had lost both her parents and was being raised by her cousin, Mordecai. It doesn't sound like these girls had a choice; and for some, they probably had to be taken by force, kicking and screaming. But for many, the thought of the chance of being queen could have been quite exciting.

Esther was given special food and beauty treatments for a whole year, and she was placed into the best place in the harem. She was a favorite, for sure. During this time, Mordecai walked back and forth near the courtyard of the harem trying to find out how Esther was and what was happening to her. Now here was a time where we should have heard the Lord's name loud and clear from Mordecai. He should have been praying instead of pacing. Mordecai had forbidden Esther to reveal that she was a Jew. It's like he knew that would be dangerous. His fear here was so obvious. You see him trying to control the situation and find a solution instead of going to the Lord.

Esther was chosen to have her night with the king. She was told that she could take anything she wanted to take with her from the harem, but she took just what her instructor told her, which was very clever. She knew that the instructor knew what pleased the king, so that would help her in pleasing the king, which was the goal. It worked! She won the king's favor and she became his queen.

Mordecai sat at the king's gate, which meant that he held a city position. As he sat in his place, he overheard a conspiracy to assassinate the king. He got word of it to Esther, who in turn reported it to the king, giving credit to Mordecai. And when the report was investigated and found to be true, the two officials were hung on gallows. All this was recorded in the book of the annals in the presence of the king. It was all according to protocol. But all the while, it was still a part of God's perfect timing and plan.

The king had a man named Haman, who was second in command, and he loved that position more than you can even imagine. All the royal officials would kneel down and pay honor to him when he walked by—except Mordecai. When asked why, Mordecai told them that he was a Jew. I give him credit for admitting that he was a Jew, but here is another time when God's name should have been proclaimed and honored. He had a chance to be bold and testify to only one God, but he didn't. He just said that he was a Jew. That was not enough explanation in my opinion.

Haman was enraged, to say the least. He decided that not only would he kill Mordecai, but he would also destroy all Mordecai's people, the Jews, throughout the whole kingdom. He had to get permission from the king for that, so when he went to present the idea, he even offered to pay for the cost that would accumulate for those who would carry out this mission. The king couldn't care less. He didn't know the Jews, and he didn't care about the Jews. So he took his signet ring from his finger and gave it to Haman. He told him to keep his money and go ahead and seal the deal. He said that Haman could do with the people as he pleased. So a specific day was set that this would be carried out, and the plan on that day was to annihilate all the Jews—the young and old, women and little children.

When Mordecai learned of all of this, he tore his clothes, put on sackcloth and ashes, went out into the city, and wailed loudly and bitterly. Here again, what an opportunity to mention the Lord's name. What a sight he was! What a racket he made. What a spectacle! He should have been on his knees pleading with the Lord and submitting to His will. When the order went out to all the provinces, the Bible says that the people went into great mourning, with fasting, weeping and wailing. Yes, they fasted, but not fasted and PRAYED. Many people fast for many reasons. It doesn't necessarily mean it's a religious act. So all the Jews' actions were far from demonstrating a confidence in their God. God's name should have been ringing out from every Jewish home. In fact, I would have thought that at this time they would have realized they had made a huge mistake by staying in Persia, and felt they should have been back in Jerusalem. They would have had to be working hard, but they would have been alive. But there is no hint of that at all. Maybe you think that I am cruel and insensitive right about now, but this is the behavior of those who do not know who their God is. What about the words that God gave to Joshua, that are ours today, about NEVER leaving us or forsaking us? What about the words of the Psalmist who said that God is our refuge and strength—our ever present help in our time of trouble? Crises hit all of us. None of us volunteer for them, but our actions in the surprises of life truly reflect the condition of our hearts. It truly reflects who has control of our hearts. It shows how much we dare surrender, by faith, to God's will. Our testimony and love for our Lord is demonstrated to others the most when we are going through the hard times rather than the good ones. Mordecai's behavior did NOT reflect faith in his God. He was scared to death because he did not know what God was capable of doing. Fear will replace peace every time when you DON'T know your God. But the flip side is so wonderful. Your fear can turn to peace when you DO know your God.

When Esther heard about how Mordecai was acting, she sent him new clothes. Come on, new clothes? This is another time the Lord's name should have been out there—not new clothes! When she found out that he did not accept the clothes, she ordered a servant to find out what was troubling him. When the word got back to her, Mordecai urged her to go into the king's presence to beg for mercy and plead with him for her people. Oh, NOW, when there is no other choice, admit that she is a Jew. Esther knew there was no way she could waltz into the king's presence without an invitation. If she did, she could be killed. She sent that message back to Mordecai—sorry, not a good idea. Then Mordecai came back with the most profound words from the Lord. However, he didn't even realize Who they were from. *"And who knows but that you have come to royal position for such a time as this?"* ✞ (4:14b.)

Those were great words of advice. They are true. But it was another time that the Lord's name should have been oozing all over here. It's like Mordecai knew that the Jews would be spared, but he just didn't know how. So he thought it had to be through Esther and him. He was carrying this unbelievable pressure that all of the Jewish nation which was left in Persia depended on Esther and him. Sometimes I think that we all try to control situations. We forget Who is God. Without even realizing it, we have pushed Him off the throne of our lives and got on that throne ourselves, thinking that we know how to handle this problem and will do it our way. And when we are on the throne of our own lives, the Lord's name won't be mentioned, either.

For the sake of her people, and from the pressure of Mordecai making her believe that it's all up to her, she was willing to go before the king. As GOD would have it, the king accepted her into his presence, and she was given anything she wanted from him, up to half the kingdom. You have to read the small, but full of adventure, book of Esther. You can picture the banquets that she so cunningly gave. You see the arrogance of Haman. You see how the king couldn't sleep and wanted the annals read to him. He realized that Mordecai was never rewarded for his heroism. You see how Haman's plan backfired. You can't help but see the hand of God's providence steering and driving in just the right direction. Haman was destroyed and Mordecai took his place in the kingdom. Esther was the heroine, and the Jews were saved. The Jews even celebrate this day every year because Mordecai said to, not the Lord. I went back to Exodus and found that the Lord told Moses to tell the people to celebrate the Passover every year so that they would always remember how the LORD delivered them from the bondage of the Egyptians. In the book of Esther, the Lord is not mentioned or given credit at all. In fact, in the last chapter of Esther, not only is the Lord not given credit, but it is all about the greatness of Mordecai and all that he did for the good of his people. There is no mention that the Jews in Persia went back to Jerusalem. They stayed there where it was comfortable. Mordecai was placed in a powerful position, Esther remained queen of a pagan nation, and none of them mentioned what GOD had done.

Maybe one may say that they stayed there to be a witness. Then my question is, "How can you be a witness for someone when you do not even mention their name?"

Why is the book of Esther written without His name even mentioned? I believe with all my heart, it's a book of warning. It's a book of grace. It shows how easy it is to get lax in our faith, and because of that we try to control our lives and people around us. It's a warning to know Who your God is and Who is the ultimate Commander and Chief. It's a book of grace, because when we don't deserve it, the Lord steps in and saves—first with salvation, and every second thereafter, from ourselves.

As I have studied the Psalms, I see the Psalmist prove how great God is and there is no other, and this great God gives us all a choice whether we want to believe in Him or not. This great God simply points out the consequences of each choice (Psalms 1, 2, 8). Then see how they prove that this great God is personal (Psalms 23, 46, 51, 91, 136, and 139). I also see how they prove that God is our helper in our time of need (Psalms 27, 119, and 121). Finally, the Psalmist expresses over and over how much the Lord loves praise and how worthy He is of it all (Psalms 34, 145, 146, 147, 148, 149, and 150).

If you will take the time and read those Psalms in their entirety, I think you will see how perfectly the Lord knows us. He knows we need to be led. He knows we need to feel safe. He knows that we need to be cleansed and forgiven. He knows that we need to hear how we need Him over and over. He, and He alone, is the only One who can do and be all that we need, and He loves to do it. However, the Psalms have shown clearly that He also loves, deserves, and is worthy of our praise. After all that God had done for Mordecai and Esther, why, oh, why didn't they praise Him for all that He had done through them? At the end of the book of Esther, why did they take all the glory? If they really were walking close to Him, they would have praised Him. Praise comes naturally the more you know who He is and how He works in us. *Now to him who is able to do immeasurably more than all we ask or imagine, according to his power that is at work within us* (Ephesians 3:20).

If you will choose to believe every word of those Psalms, you will experience God in a way that you can't help but mention, share, shout, and proclaim HIS NAME! ✟ His Name is above all names, worthy to be PRAISED. May there NEVER be a chapter in the book of our lives where you and I do not mention His Name!

God is the hero of the Old Testament. Yes, He used many people, but HE was, is, and always will be the REAL HERO of the universe, the world, and I pray, your life and mine.

CHAPTER 12

JESUS'   SIGNPOSTS

"Promised Land": ✞ Pg. 264

●...Hebrews 10:36-39, *You need to persevere so that when you have done the will of God, you will receive what he has promised. For in just a very little while, "He who is coming will come and will not delay.*
But my righteous one will live by faith. And if he shrinks back, I will not be pleased with him." But we are not of those who shrink back and are destroyed, but of those who believe and are saved.

●...John 14:2-4, *In my Father's house are many rooms; if it were not so, I would have told you. I am going there to prepare a place for you. And if I go and prepare a place for you, I will come back and take you to be with me that you also may be where I am. You know the way to the place where I am going."*

"Scripture God-Breathed": ✞ Pg. 265

●...2 Timothy 3:16-17, *All Scripture is God-breathed and is useful for teaching, rebuking, correcting and training in righteousness, so that the man of God may be thoroughly equipped for every good work.*

● ...John 1:1, *In the beginning was the Word* [Jesus] *and the Word was with God, and the Word was God. He was with God in the beginning.*

● ...Revelation 19:13, *He* [Jesus] *is dressed in a robe dipped in blood, and his name is the Word of God.*

"Time as This": ✝ Pg. 270

● ...John 5:17, *Jesus said to them, "My Father is always at his work to this very day, and I, too, am working."*

● ...Luke 18:27, *Jesus replied, "What is impossible with men is possible with God."*

"His Name": ✝ Pg. 272

● ...Philippians 2:9-11, *Therefore God exalted him to the highest place and gave him the name that is above every name, that at the name of Jesus every knee should bow, in heaven and on earth and under the earth, and every tongue confess that Jesus Christ is Lord, to the glory of God the Father.*

Lesson 12: The End of Captivity, Queen Esther, and God's Providence
Esther

1. According to Jeremiah 29:10-14, where did God want his people to be when the captivity was over?

2. If they would have all gone back when they were suppose to, would the Book of Esther even have been necessary? Do you believe that God has a perfect and permissive will? Why is it so much smarter to strive for staying in His perfect will?

3. In this book, you see God's grace, and once again He uses human beings to fulfill a promise that He is determined to keep. Who does God use in this book to do that, even though neither will proclaim His name?

4. What kind of environment did the Jews have in Persia? Why did they like it so much? Why do you think that they chose to stay there instead of going back?

5. What do you like about Queen Vashti?

6. What was Mordecai's state of mind when Esther was taken to the palace? (2:11). What should it have been if he had had a right relationship with his God? (Philippians 4:6-7.)

7. Why was Esther chosen to be queen? (The answer is NOT only because she was beautiful. Who made her beautiful, anyway?)

8.   What was Haman's plot? How did Mordecai and the Jews handle the news? (4:1-3.) What should they have done?

9.   What did Mordecai tell Esther to do?

10.   How did it all turn out? (2: 21-23 and chapters 6-8.)

11.   Who took it upon himself to create a holiday? (9: 20-23, 27-28.) Compare this to the Lord's instructions in Exodus 12.

12.   Who is the last chapter of Esther all about? Considering all God had done, does this settle right with you?

13.   Do you get the impression that Mordecai and Esther thought that they had pulled this salvation off on their own? Is there anything a human being can do to save themselves?

14.   When you have been saved from your sin, self, God's wrath, judgment, and hell, whose Name will you shout out? (There is only One answer here.) Doesn't it disturb you that you never hear His Name in the book of Esther?

15.   Who is the ONLY Hero in the Book of Esther?

16.   Finally, after not having much to work with during 400 years of silence between Malachi and Matthew, what does John the Baptist proclaim in Matthew 3:1-3?

17.   How does your old life become new? Who is the only One who can turn old into new? Praise the Lord!

Closing Remarks

The Old Testament closes with the prophet Malachi warning the people of the great final Day of Judgment. For those who are committed to God, judgment day will be a day of joy because it will usher in eternity in God's presence. Those who have ignored God will be "stubble" to be burned. In the very last two verses of the Old Testament, Malachi prophesied that before the final judgment God would send a prophet like Elijah who would prepare the way for Jesus, the Messiah. That man was John the Baptist.

From the time of the last prophet's prophesy until the time of John the Baptist was 400 years. That was a LONG period of silence. The Israelites were promised a Messiah, and then there was that long span of WAITING. Why did God do that? Why did He make them wait, and why does He make us wait sometimes? Why doesn't He always answer right away? What is the purpose of waiting? The questions are endless when it comes to why God makes His children wait. Waiting isn't a waste of time; it is God's prime time in which He is getting everything ready. It also can be a test to see if we will really trust and know that His timing is perfect, and NOT jump ahead and miss His blessing, which always follows. It's the reward for waiting. So when He isn't answering quickly enough for you, remember, He is up to something. He never wastes time. He holds time in His hands, so we trust His timing.

The New Testament begins with Matthew presenting the genealogy of Jesus. This genealogy revealed the Old Testament timeline by showing that Jesus was a descendent of Abraham, the father of all Jews, and a direct descendant of David, fulfilling the Old Testament prophesy to the letter. I love the way God uses five women in Jesus' line. Ordinary women like you and me. Women who have had "pasts." Women who dared to step out and believe with a simple faith and accept His forgiveness, and then offer themselves back to Him as living sacrifices. He isn't as concerned about what we have been as about what we choose to do with Him and whether we allow Him to turn us into what He created us to be. In Matthew 3, John the Baptist begins his ministry by calling the people to turn from their sins and to turn toward God. *"Repent, for the kingdom of heaven is near."* He quoted from the Old Testament prophet, Isaiah: *A voice of one calling: "In the desert prepare the way for the LORD; make straight in the wilderness a highway for our God"* (Isaiah 40:3).

As you can see, the Old Testament has now transitioned into the New Testament; Jesus was coming! It's because of Jesus coming to fulfill His mission at the Cross that we, too, can be transitioned from the old to the new. *Therefore, if anyone is in Christ, he is a new creation; the old has gone, the new has come!* (II Corinthians 5:17.)

And with this new creation, comes a new look. *And we, who with unveiled faces all reflect the Lord's glory, are being transformed into his likeness with ever-increasing glory, which comes from the Lord, who is the Spirit* (II Corinthians 3:18).

At our resurrection, we are promised that our old bodies will be transformed into new ones, just like Jesus'. God will give us a transformed eternal body that will be perfect for our eternal life. *And just as we have borne the likeness of the earthly man, so shall we bear the likeness of the man from heaven* (I Corinthians 15:49).

And finally, at the end of time, there is another change from old to new. *Then I saw a new heaven and a new earth, for the first heaven and the first earth had passed away...."* (Revelation 21:1a.)

So, you see, God turns old into new. Now open your "eyes" and watch Him work. His transforming power has a way of changing the universe, the world, and you and me. And when He turns old into new, well, like Genesis 1 said numerous times after each one of His new creations, "IT WAS GOOD!" IT'S ALWAYS GOOD!

15681007R00150

Made in the USA
Charleston, SC
15 November 2012